"Besides being chock-f
who speaks needs to k
making whatever he ta
could write two hundred pages on dryer lint and hold my attention. Have your highlighting pen ready; you'll be referring back to this book time and again."

— *Lewis Harrison, Past President of the
National Speakers Association, New York Chapter*

"This 'Top Ten' format is easy and fun to follow, as Milo coaches you through with tips, ideas and strategies you can use right away. He has compiled a full spectrum of information any presenter needs to be brilliant."

— *Sheryl Roush, international speaker, trainer, author,
Past President San Diego Professional Coaches Alliance,
Past District Governor, Toastmasters International*

"Milo provides what you need to know about public speaking and then some. A one-stop read for new and experienced public speakers. The illustrations and examples make it fun to read!!"

— *Barbara Greenstein, Past Pres. of the American Society
of Training & Development, San Diego Chapter*

"Milo Shapiro's 'Public Speaking: Get A's, Not Zzzzzz's!' is a must read for people who are serious about public speaking. It's like a cafeteria with morsels of wisdom that can satisfy any level of 'speaking appetite' - from novice to advanced. Let Milo's years of hands-on speaking experience help you advance your speaking skills."

— *Stuart Burkow, co-author of* **"Guerrilla Profits"**,
President, Guerrilla Profits Int'l (www.GuerrillaProfits.com)

"Speak!"

— Milo Shapiro

David,

Enjoy + thanks for the support!

Milo

Public Speaking:

Get A's, Not ZZZzzz's!

A fun and helpful guide to being prepared, polished, and powerful

By Milo Shapiro
www.IMPROVentures.com

Illustrations within by Bob Teitelbaum
Cover drawing by Jorge Pacheco

Published by Lulu

Public Speaking…Get A's, Not Zzzzzz's!

First Edition

©2008, Milo Shapiro

All rights reserved. Published by Lulu. www.lulu.com , Morrisville, NC.

No portion of this book may be reproduced or transmitted in any form or by any means, electronic or mechanical, including photocopying, without permission in writing from the author. For such permission, especially in the context of review, contact the author directly through his website, www.IMPROVentures.com.

All illustrations in this book are the property of Milo Shapiro, as contracted from Jorge Pacheco and Robert Teitelbaum.

ISBN: 978-1-4303-1236-9 (pbk)

Library of Congress Control Number: 2007906084
    Public Speaking…Get A's, Not Zzzzzz's!

Printed in the United States of America.

DEDICATION

To my Dad:

*For all that we know
you've done for us...*

*And so many more things that we'll
never know that you've done for us...*

Much love and appreciation!

Hope the book makes you proud.

Table of Contents

Chapter		Page
0	Introduction	11
0½	The Power of Story	15
1	Ten Things To Know and Do Before You Even Start To Plan	19
2	Ten Sensible Things To Do To Be Ready For A Specific Event	39
3	Ten Things You Can Wear To Distract or Annoy An Audience	57
4	Ten Things To Do When You First Arrive	65
5	Ten Helpful Things To Do In The Time Between Your "Arrival Stuff" and Going Onstage	73
6	Ten Survival Tips Regarding Introductions	85
7	Ten Considerations About What Your Introduction Should(n't) Include	93
8	Ten Great Ways To Blow It In Your First Ten Seconds	99
9	Ten Bonus Ways To Blow It In Your First *Thirty* Seconds	103
10	Ten Neat Things To Talk About If You WANT To Alienate Your Audience	111
11	Ten More Things You Can Do To Alienate Your Audience	117
12	Ten Great Ways to Blow It With Visuals	125
13	Ten Hot Tips for Handouts	131
14	Ten Sensible Ways to Organize Your Program	139

Chapter		Page
15	Ten Smart Ways to Maximize Your PowerPoint Experience	145
16	Ten Gold Nuggets for Rehearsing	153
17	Ten Cool Tricks to Ease the Torture of Memorization	161
18	Ten Insiders Secrets for the Best Use of Your Voice	169
19	Ten Healing Ways to Deal With The FEAR and Reduce the STRESS	175
20	Ten Ideas for Dealing With Q&A	185
21	Ten Crucial Techniques for Pacing Time	193
22	Ten Superb Reasons To Join Toastmasters or Hire a Speaking Coach	201
23	Ten Steps to Making the Leap to Getting Speeches	207
24	Ten Steps to Making the Leap to Getting *Paid* for Speeches	221
25	Epilogue (or 10 Final Thoughts on Speaking)	231

Appendix A: Check list to prepare for speech	233
Appendix B: Packing check list for all travel	235
Appendix C: Packing check list for speaking	237
Acknowledgements	238
About the Author	239
About the Illustrator	245

0
Introduction

Who is this guy?
And why should I read <u>this</u> book?

*(especially when there are lots
of other books on this topic!)*

Good questions! I know the answer to the first one for sure – I'm practically an expert on that. So let's come back to who I am. Only you can answer the second one and since the answer could be "I don't need to read this book," let's take a look at the options.

Foremost: Is your house on fire? If so, then you should deal with that first. Good public speaking is important, but it won't save your life. And this book is flammable, which will only add to the problem. Quite frankly, I don't have enough insurance to deal with the implications of that.

Second: Do you prefer books that consider themselves to be V.I.B.'s? Because this book is not a V.I.B. V.I.B.'s are "Very Important Books." They're the kind of books you want to *have read* but you don't exactly want to sit down and *read*. In high school, these were books like *Long Day's Journey Into Night* and *Moby Dick*. I'd love to say that I'd read them, but in truth there was always some sitcom I wanted to watch more.

As adults, there are V.I.B.'s, too. They usually have titles like:

> *"On Being Productive Through Goal
> Setting and Time Management"*

Doesn't that sound like a book you'd benefit from *having read?* Sure. But does it sound like something you would honestly want to sit down and *read?* Well, I don't know you, but I have a funny feeling that about nine pages into it, my mind would be off in

Tahiti — without me. I prefer to read something that speaks to me in a way that reflects how I like to think.

Likewise, in spite of my own passion for public speaking, I've seen too many V.I.B.'s on the topic that could put a person to sleep immediately after drinking a full Starbucks® Venti Mocha. And that's a shame! To my way of thinking, speaking in public is inherently *interesting*! It's about exciting people regarding a message that you want or need to share. It's exposing people to new ideas and possibly motivating them to take action. So why do so many books on the topic suck the life out of it? Why can't they be fun and stimulating reading and still be packed with content?

If you've survived these first five paragraphs, you've already realized that I don't write like most other training authors. I prefer to write the same way that I would speak to you — which, oddly enough, I think is valuable if the topic at hand is *how to speak to people!*

I'll try to keep things light to make sure that this book is a comfortable and fun read, but not at the expense of saying what needs to be said.

I also strongly believe that we can tell people facts until their heads are swimming, but if you tell a good story with a lesson built in, the message resonates and sticks. For this reason, I illustrate a lot of my points with examples and tales. Some come from times when following this advice caused a positive outcome, but many are those lessons learned through trial-by-fire. A good number of my anecdotes come from personally having lived out some foul-up…and surviving to write it down (and we DO survive them all) so that you never have to experience the same problem.

If my speaking style sounds too informal for the type of speaking you might do, let me share a few thoughts with you:

1. I want this book to be fun to learn from. It doesn't mean I *always* speak informally. It's just one possible approach and it's the one I chose for this book.

2. Some people reading this book (maybe you, maybe not) may think that speaking to a group is scarier than bungee jumping off a space shuttle. So just *reading* a book on speaking to an audience may have their stomach in a knot. If I can keep this book a little lighter, maybe it'll help those people to keep breathing, thinking…and reading.

3. With each passing year, a higher percentage of the audiences we address are made up of Generation X (born 1965 – 1980), Generation Y (born 1981 – 1994), and even Millenials (born 1995 or later). These are folks who do not remember life before MTV, America's Funniest Videos, and reality TV. They are far more used to learning from an informal approach than Baby Boomers and the generation before them. Including the right percentage of informality holds their attention better.

4. My speaking engagements have been well-received by professional organizations such as Minolta, Pfizer, Kodak, Southwest Airlines, Hilton Hotels, the American Society of

Training and Development, and the Project Management Institute. Something I'm doing seems to be working.

5. You're still reading the introduction, which is probably a good sign.

With the long-running success of David Letterman's "Top Ten" lists and their many parodies, I decided that this would be a fun format to use for discussing the many lessons around presentation skills and public speaking (these two terms are often used interchangeably, but are not always the same).

Since this isn't a VIB, I encourage you to mark up this book so it's an easy reference tool. On your first reading, circle with pencil areas that you think you'll want to come back to when you're ready to act upon them. Write ideas that come to you in the margin as you read.

Most importantly, highlight points that you think you might want to be able to quickly find to reconsider right before an event. Only you know which ones are best for you, be it packing tips or fear reduction ideas or reminders on what to do when you arrive…whatever suits *your* needs.

After you finish, when the time comes for you to do a presentation, a simple ten-minute review of the highlighted bullet points will be like having all those lessons rush back to you without having to re-read the book.

Though you're always welcome to!

0½
The Power of Story

If you read the intro, you know that I believe strongly in the power of **story** as a tool for speaking and teaching.

Most of your audiences will be mature enough that they can learn from you *without* the use of story, so why do I take the time to mention it in the introduction *and* add this special bonus chapter just to emphasize this point? Because I firmly believe that nothing else you do in your attempts to become a better speaker will help you more than becoming a good story teller *and* selecting the right stories to support your intentions. (Just like on "American Idol"; how many times has Simon Cowell bemoaned, "Decent job, but you sang the wrong song for you." You've gotta tell the *right* stories or it won't matter how well you tell them!)

Here are just a few reasons why I'm dedicated to helping people integrate these skills into their presentations:

Memory

Story is proven to be an effective means of getting listeners to absorb and remember the idea you wish to share,.

If I asked you to tell me the five most important lessons you learned from a parent, you might be able to do it, but I'm guessing it would take some thought.

By contrast, if I asked you to tell me the moral of these five stories:

1. The Hare and the Tortoise
2. The Boy Who Cried Wolf
3. The Mouse and the Thorn in the Lion's Paw
4. Green Eggs and Ham
5. The Wizard of Oz

...most readers could rattle off something like:

1. Slow and steady wins the race.
2. If you tell lies, no one will believe the truth.
3. Even the smallest creatures can be good allies.
4. You have to try new things.
5. There's no place like home.

And even if you missed one (or worded the lesson slightly different than I did), chances are the whole story came rushing back to you when you saw the moral I listed.

Now which are more important in most of our lives: the influence of our parents or "The Hare and the Tortoise"? For most, it'd be our parents, yet "Slow and steady wins the race" is a stronger memory for us. ***That's*** the power of story. And that's the power I want *you* to bring to your presentations...with lessons people will not just follow, but *remember.* And when they remember the lesson with the story, they will remember ***you*** along with it.

Attention

The brain seems to process stories in a different way than it does facts. For whatever reason, there is a great sense of relief in hearing a story by comparison. This is the reason that a good sermon is usually the highlight of a religious service. Rather than merely reciting the rules, expectations, and devotional comments, we are now treated to a tale. Be it from the Bible, current events, or a childhood story of the orator, we are taken someplace else and given the opportunity to visualize something being played out. We are taken on a journey that lands us back where we started, but wiser for the trip.

We like to believe that we are far grown up from the children who gathered on the floor around the school librarian's feet, as she opened up a tome from the bookshelf. But the reality is that we turn from such tales to Hollywood and let *them* tell us stories where the visuals are simply given to us. As adults, we relish stories just as much; we just like them to be a little richer.

New parents often rediscover this joy when they start to read bedtime stories to their children. One friend admitted to me that she was looking forward to bedtime that night so she could find out what was going to happen next in the story she was reading to her son.

Never under-estimate the power of story!

When you create good stories and tell them well, you will have your audiences fully present and more than willing to give you their complete attention.

Impact

"…when I read the good news, my first instinct was to call Jim to tell him what happened. He'd be so excited. My hand was halfway to the phone before it hit me, as it had hit me over a dozen times that week, that Jim had passed away. He was gone. There would be no telling Jim about anything anymore. No calls. No notes. No visits. No laughing. No shoulder. And the grieving would start over, again and again, in moments like these, as the reality slowly sunk in."

Nothing has the power to evoke emotion or personalize a message more quickly or powerfully than a story. In only a few lines of typing, I took you to another place and time in my life, back in the mid-nineties, when my emotions were strong and I was learning some lessons that I would share later. Whether we are sharing bad times or good, personal tales or those of the world, stories give us far more opportunity to make a strong impression upon those we are addressing.

For the reasons we've just gone over, you'll find that I will use stories in this book to make my points as well.

Now that we've made that point, let's start working with our top ten lists so everything else about our speeches, from advanced preparation to leaving the stage, will be top-notch.

Come on…it'll be fun!

1

10 Things To Know and Do Before You Even *Start* To Plan For A Specific Event

Don't get me wrong: I love the excitement of improvisation and the rush that comes from the risk it involves. I even love adlibbing a bit in my keynote speeches when something relates to the room or when I can make a tie-in to something that preceded me. But these are situations where I'm in control. The last thing I want when I'm speaking is surprises...especially when I could have headed them off by being better prepared!

While there is an entire art and skill set to handling those times when we need to speak unexpectedly, most of the time we are forewarned when we are to make a presentation.

What can you do to start preparing *right now* for the possibility that you might be asked to speak at some point? This might seem like an odd question, but if you expect that you will be doing some speaking, there are steps you can take now to be a few steps ahead of the game.

1. **Have a question list that you'll go through every time you talk to a meeting planner.**

This has been one of the most valuable tools I've ever incorporated into my business.

When I first entered the business, I was winging it every time, assuming that the meeting planner would provide all the information I'd need. I learned quickly that there were things I needed to ask or the information would never reach me. As I'd subsequently call back to get answers to issues I *should* have asked up front, two things happened:

1) I looked unprepared and unprofessional.
2) I inevitably forgot to ask one or two things I should have before arriving.

By creating a **Question List**, you ensure that you never forget anything and you show your level of detail and competence to the planner. Once the speaking engagement seems likely, I officially switch into ~~the~~ Interview Mode. I'll usually say something like:

"Maggie, over the years I've compiled a list of questions about upcoming speaking engagements. It'll take us about five to ten minutes to get through, depending upon your answers. I know that this may sound like a lot, but each question on the list comes from an experience when I realized, belatedly, that I would have more prepared for the event had I asked.

"By the time we finish this survey, there shouldn't be any chance that there will be topics we *should have* covered. Can you spend that time right now to go through the questions with me?"

Rarely have I had someone say no because if they are taking the time to try to get me the information, five to ten minutes is negligible to ensure that it's done right.

On the rare occasion where someone says that they cannot spare the time, I counter with:

"These are questions that I *will* need the answers to so that I can do my best work for you. Since you can't spare the time right now, can I just ask you the most critical ones and send you the rest to answer by e-mail?"

I've never had any reaction to this other than a yes or a simple rescheduling, sometimes by phone. Why *wouldn't* they want you to do your best?

Have a question list that you'll go through every times you talk to a meeting planner

Once in a while, someone will comment that there were more questions than they expected, but they almost always add, "But these are good questions — I'm glad you asked!" or "That's something we haven't been asked before but I'm sure I can find out for you. Just asking the questions can often cause the planner to give more thought to what outcome or arrangement he wants to make for the event...and you've done that person a favor.

Your needs will not be identical to mine so I *want* your questionnaire to be customized for your events. I have included my current question list in Appendix A for you to look over, but I recommend that you visit my website for a live version. You can copy and paste from that one to begin editing the copy that will be all yours. Most importantly, every time you realize that there is a question you *wish* you had asked, add it to your list! The list I've provided is the result of three years of continual growth.

The online list as I created for myself can be found on the resource link at **www.IMPROVentures.com** and is yours for free with this book.

2. Have a checklist for packing for that day.

Ever go on a vacation and forget to pack a belt because you didn't need one on the pants you were wearing that day? Wouldn't it be nice to have a list where you just check off all likely items, so you can't forget something as commonplace as a belt or slippers or your camera?

Years ago, I made up a list for just that purpose and it has saved my butt many times. I even include items that only apply to certain kinds of trips, like flashlights, bug spray, and gloves. It's easy enough to cross those off when they don't apply.

Just like traveling on a vacation, there are certain tools one is likely to want when one is addressing a group. While my list may not be identical to yours, an excellent starting place is the list I have included in Appendix B for you. I'm also adding the ordinary travel list as Appendix C, in case you might find that helpful. Heck, it doesn't cost me anything to add it, so why not? We're all friends here.

Both of these lists are also on the web resource page mentioned in item 1, if you'd like to create a personalized version or just print it each time so you can cross off as you pack.

3. Have your own name badge.

This is one of the many places in this book where the advice is good, but only for those for whom it applies. If you are making presentations to your co-workers, especially ones you see frequently, a name tag is only going to look dorky, so forget it.

By contrast, many of us in business are meeting new people all the time — at mixers, business functions, conferences, and more. Why would you want people's first impression of your identity to be a "***Hello My Name Is***..." sticker that you penned your name onto at the card table by the door?

Arrive with your pre-made name tag that will look more professional than what can be made at the door with a marker.

Or worse: Using one of those pre-printed name cards that go into a slot where they've put their organization's name and logo in big letters, but your name and company are way smaller and harder to read?

Or the very worst: The "just put your business card in here and pin the holder to yourself" concept. Now you have to hope that anyone who might have used your services can read your card in an eight point font on your moving body. Absurd!

The solution is so simple and will cost you nothing. Find one of those clear 3"x4" plastic name tag holders that every convention gives out hundreds of (you've probably thrown away dozens over the years). Go to your computer and design a name tag that will fit in the holder and will look **exactly** the way you want it to.

With 3"x4", you have more than enough room to put your name, company logo, company name, and even a little slogan to intrigue people.

This has been of great value for me at networking events, especially when someone wearing the routine "Hello My Name Is…" sticker says to me: "That's a good idea. I like your name tag. So what exactly *is* IMPROVentures?" That sets me up nicely to tell them about my company and where the name came from. And that's why I'm there in the first place — to have conversations that lead to exactly that discussion.

A good name tag can help you immediately show people what you have to offer.

For a little more money, you can have one professionally made, but I've been happy with mine and if I lose it (and I do), I simply print out a new one.

---

4. Have a template for your introduction.

Before I start this section, I have to clarify what I mean by the word "introduction":

In grade school, we were taught that anything we wrote had to have an introduction, a body, and a conclusion. While that's not untrue, in the world of speaking, we refer to an *opening*, a body, and a conclusion because the word introduction has a separate meaning.

The introduction refers to the words someone *else* says about you *before* you take the focus. The intention is the let the audience know a little bit about you so they know why you are their speaker.

The introduction should, at the very least, give the audience some comfort that you have credentials that make it clear why you'll be addressing them. Ideally, it should also pique their interest so that they will look forward to hearing what you have to say.

A well-crafted introduction is almost as much of an art as a well-crafted speech. This is why you should invest a fair amount of time into writing an introduction that will serve you well.

To be sure, there will be times when you will want to customize it because audiences can vary. The goal for now is not to write the perfect introduction that would suit every time you speak. It is to create a good template that you can alter for each occasion if you see a reason to.

You may be thinking, "An introduction? That would be way too formal for what I'll be doing!" Not necessarily.

When speaking to very small groups, such as a sales presentation for five people at a conference table, a fully-read three minute introduction might feel awkward. That doesn't mean the introduction process should be skipped, though. It just means it should be done differently and shorter. In this example, it would be entirely appropriate for someone who knows the client to say:

"At this time, I'd like to turn the presentation over to Bob Hunt. He's been with us here at HugeCorp for six years and has been focused full-time for the last three years on the issues we'll be discussing today. We've asked him to create some proposals around your specific needs and I think you'll be surprised how easily they can be implemented. Bob?"

Now that shouldn't be awkward for either Bob or the clients to sit through, should it? In about twenty seconds, it gently sets Bob up to be the authority that the clients should give their attention to for a while. In essence, it sets Bob up for success. So why leave that to fate?

There will be more on introductions in later top ten lists, so finish this book for more ideas before you start writing, but know that there's no reason to wait for your next speaking opportunity to put together your template introduction.

---

5.   Get appropriate clothing.

We'll talk later about what "appropriate" means for different situations, but once you know what's appropriate, you can start shopping now to have the right look.

---

6.   Check your general look; do you look like someone they'll take seriously?

For the record, I salute your right to individuality. I think those seven piercings on your left ear look tremendous. I think the tattoo of Donald Duck on your forearm is great work. And I don't think you should have to pluck your uni-brow to please someone else's standards of beauty.

But…

As one of the stories in my book "The Worst Days Make The Best Stories" shows: You can make a choice that you will do something or take on a certain look to express yourself, but the contract you are making with the universe is that you are accepting the ramifications of your choice…including any feelings you bring up in others.

Only you can decide where the border is in your choices. One person might be very comfortable in a full conservative suit. Another might feel that he would be *selling his soul* to go a single day without his nose ring. Or without her plunging neckline. Or by wearing long sleeve simply to cover a tattoo.

But…

If you do make that choice, be cognizant that there will be people who will make judgments about what they think of your choices. Can you afford to be a martyr to prove to them that people who dress in a more extreme way should be taken seriously? Again, only you can decide that.

The bottom line: Make such choices very consciously because, if your intention is to persuade, you'll be fighting uphill to impress people who may be predisposed against a non-traditional choice.

Check your general look; do you appear like someone they'll take seriously?

---

7. **Know the advantages, disadvantages, and ways to maximize each of the most likely room set-ups.**

There are five common ways that event planners tend to set up a room for a speaker. Sometimes, they are open to discussing your options. More often, they will tell you the configuration and you will have to adapt.

Here are the main five set-ups and some considerations for each:

<u>**Theater Style**</u>

Chairs will be in rows and columns.

Advantages: You get everyone close to you so they see every facial expression you make and you can see them better, allowing you to feel more connected. If humor is used, an audience will always laugh more in a tighter space because the laughter of some gives permission to others. Everyone is facing your direction.

Disadvantages: No place for attendees to write because there are no tables. No place, except at their feet, for attendees to put any items. Little room for anyone to move around if that would help you in any interactive work you might include. Latecomers could have to move in front of on-timers to get to open seats, like at a movie.

Note: Theater Style may or may not include an aisle up the middle. This is something you often can ask for if it was not planned. I like an aisle because I tend to go out into the audience and it gives me easier access to people in the back. Also, latecomers will be more likely to sit in the center where you want them. But it does move everyone away from you by about two seat's worth to the sides in order to add an aisle.

Classroom Style

This consists of long straight tables where attendees sit on one side of the table facing you. Many college lecture halls are set up this way.

Advantages: People can write and put their belongings down. Everyone faces you.

Disadvantages: All of those tables can act as psychological barriers between you and the attendees. Each person is safely tucked in and guarded behind an obstacle. The set-up rarely includes an aisle, so the speaker is separated from everyone — even the front row.

Rounds

Eight to ten people sit around each table. This means that at least half are not facing you, probably due to a meal being served or previous activity requiring those at the table to face each other.

Advantages: Client can get the most people fed in a limited space. Note that this is an advantage to the client and the caterer, not to you. Yet it is one of the most commonly used set ups for this reason so you should anticipate it. Tables are useful, though, if you wish to have the clients writing.

Disadvantages: If there are ten people at the table, four are facing you, two are sideways and four have their backs to you. You have no control over how they will sit. Some will turn their chairs to face you directly. Some will watch you at whatever angle their chair is positioned. Some will sit at odd angles to look over the backs of their chairs. And, most horrifying, some will never turn around, making it clear that they are doing something else at their table so you end up competing against that. Also, for all ten people, anything on the table can be a distraction. You can probably tell this is far from my favorite set-up.

Crescents

Picture the same round tables as in the previous example, but only four to six people are put at each table so that no one has their back to you.

Advantages: Everyone is seated on the far side so the whole audience should be facing you. Very easy for someone to come in or leave if need be.

Disadvantages: This requires more tables to seat the same number of people, which means the people who might have had their backs to you in Rounds are now facing you, but from much further back, disconnecting them from your energy.

U-Shape

This set-up is slightly misnamed, as it is not rounded. A better description would be "three sides of a square", though that would be a mouthful.

Tables are set up in this three sided configuration and the front is open, allowing you to speak along the missing fourth side of the square.

An occasional variation on this is that people are seated on the inside of the "U" as well and one prays that they will turn their chairs around (they usually do).

Advantages: Everyone has an unblocked "front row" type view of you, though some may be quite a distance back. A wise speaker can work this to his advantage by moving into the center of the square at times — so long as he is careful not to alienate the people on the tips of the "U" who could now see his back if he is not careful. Everyone attending can write and store possessions easily.

Disadvantages: There is still a table barrier, though at least it's just one long table, not lots of rows. The shape *can* put the center people far back, though, especially if the "U" is a long, thin rectangle instead of a square.

So which one is best?

It's not that simple. If little or no writing will be done by the participant, I'll usually ask if theater style is an option, especially if the group is small enough that we can then avoid any microphones by getting them in close.

If writing is necessary, the space, group size, and the amount of activity you'll have them doing really dictate which of the other four is best. Personally, though, classroom style is my least favorite, unless I'm planning to do more training than speaking.

---

8.   Know speaker terminology.

Here are a few terms that I sometimes find people confuse or do not know.

Lectern and Podium — I put these two together because they are the most confused words in the industry. A *lectern* is a small structure (about 4 feet high), usually wooden, upon which a speaker may put his notes. The front is usually slanted with a lip at the bottom so that notes cannot slide off.

By contrast, a *podium* is a physical structure that one stands upon to be better seen from the back of a room. You can think of the word podium as the speaker's equivalent to a *stage*. Podiums may be as small as 3' x 3' or may be almost as wide as the room, which is also commonly called a *dais* (DAY-uss).

Know the correct terms of the speaking world.
We could stand ON a podium or BEHIND a lectern.

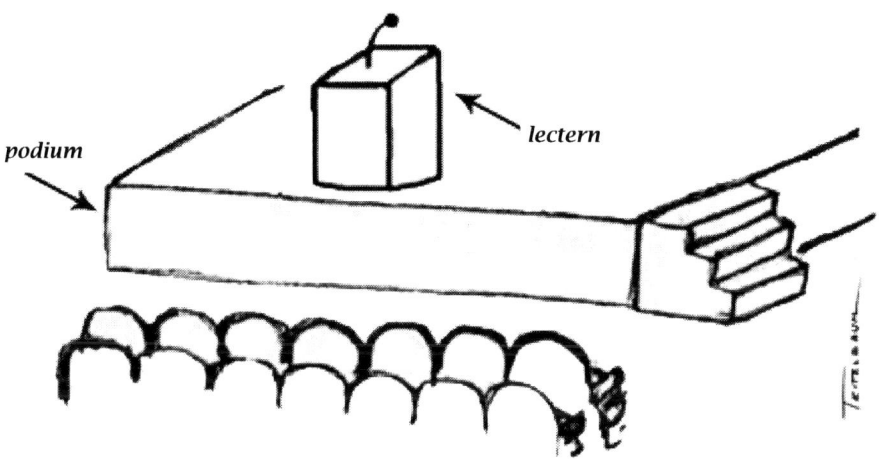

Having taught you the correct definitions now, I can also tell you that about half the people encounter will think that a lectern is called a podium.

The next word adds to the confusion:

Lavaliere (LA-vuh-LEER) — a tiny microphone for which one end is clipped onto your shirt or blouse. From there, a wire from the clipped part runs through your clothing to a power pack that clips onto a belt, waistline or pocket. The power pack broadcasts to a receiver located elsewhere in the room. Your voice is then transmitted through speakers so that you do not need to hold a microphone.

Besides the confusion between podium and lecturn, the words lavaliere and lectern are too similar for some:

An event planner told me that, of course, they'd have a *lavaliere* ready for me. Imagine my surprise when I arrived and asked about the lavaliere. She looked puzzled and said, "It's right there!" as she pointed to the *lectern*. When I explained that I was looking for amplification, she said, "Oh, there's a microphone built into that." As I am very physical in my delivery and do not work nearly as well behind a lectern, I was very fortunate that she had a small group...to whom I spoke very loudly for an hour so I wouldn't be stuck behind her misnamed object.

How do we avoid such confusion? It comes in the wording and who speaks first.

When asking about the room set up, I'll ask, "Will there be a lectern for me to put notes on?" If they say, "What's a lectern?" then I get to educate them rather than correct them when they might have used the word podium.

When I first use the word lavaliere, I always use this highly redundant question: "Will you be able to provide a lavaliere body mike so that I can have my hands free?" This way, even if the word *lavaliere* is new to the planner, she'll get the meaning by the end of the question.

A few more terms that are good to know, even if they don't fit the kind of speaking you'll be doing:

<u>Keynote</u> — This refers to a speech, generally 60 or 90 minutes, that will be the primary one at a given gathering. Likewise, the person giving it is frequently called the *keynote speaker*.

<u>Breakout</u> — This refers to a program that is being given opposite other programs where the attendees can choose the session that interests them most. The same speech that was a keynote at one conference could be a breakout session at another, depending on scheduling and planning.

<u>Signature Story</u> — This is a reference to a story that was created by the speaker which he uses in his keynotes to help prove a point. It is usually funny, poignant, or gripping in nature. Its purpose is focusing the audience's attention for the point at the end. There is no rule of thumb as to where in the program this story should appear. It is absolutely taboo to use another speaker's signature story…even if you credit that person with the material. (Thus the reference to it being his "signature".) Don't worry…you've got a million stories of your own to develop!

<u>Introduction vs. Opening</u> — An *introduction* is what someone *else* says in order to bring you on stage. As mentioned earlier, an *opening* is the first section of your speech, used to draw people's interest to the body of your speech. These terms are often incorrectly used interchangeably.

NSA — National Speakers Association. This is a professional society of people who make most or all of their living through speaking. It is not an easy organization to join, so knowing that a speaker is a member is usually a good indication of their quality.

Speakers Bureau — A business which pre-qualifies professional speakers. Event planners can contact the bureau to identify a good fits for any given topic. The bureau creates the connection and contract with the speaker in return for a percentage of the speaker's fee.

Toastmasters — An international, educational, non-profit alliance of clubs whose focus is improving the communication skills of their members. This great organization brings out friendly, positive people who support and critique other members as they take turns giving practice presentations. While a member might only speak periodically at their Toastmasters club, there is still a lot of learning that takes place by watching other speakers, followed by hearing the critique in a supportive environment.

---

9. **Be prepared to introduce who you are and what you do in an engaging manner in 15 seconds or less.**

Okay, we DO need one more vocabulary word, but it's significant enough to deserve its own top-ten point. The term is **elevator speech** and it applies to a lot more than speaking engagements.

Hopefully, no one is out there actually giving actual speeches in elevators, so let's not worry about that possibility. Why the name? An elevator speech refers to a scenario like this:

You get into an elevator on the first floor of a building along with a well-dressed woman. She says, "Good morning." You respond likewise as the doors close. She says, "I don't believe I've seen you in this building before. I'm Gayle Francis, the director of _____ here at MegaCorp."

You realize that this is a golden opportunity to introduce yourself to this powerful person. She'll be on the elevator for about 15 more seconds and the clock is ticking. What do you say so that she will respond, "Really! Do you have a card?" instead of "That's nice. Very pleasant to have met you," before she steps off at her floor?

If you haven't practiced it, chances are you aren't going to be succinct enough to get your message across to her effectively. You're looking for one to three sentences that make you seem interesting and knowledgeable in the area of your choosing. This level of brevity is also the key to sounding unrushed and less desperate than you really are.

In reality, we don't generally use our elevator speeches in situations where people will disappear in a few seconds. The goal is to be so crystal clear and fascinating in your topic that the person you are talking to will ask you to expand upon what you said.

For example, I knew a financial planner who focused on retirement plans. When someone would ask Dan's colleagues what they did for a living, most of them would say, "I'm a financial planner with MegaFinancial," and receive a response like "Oh...that's nice."

By contrast, Dan's answer was always, "I help people plan for the possibility that they may live far longer than they expected." How much more interesting is THAT to hear? Inevitably, the reaction is a question probing for more details or an empathic tale of someone *they* knew who outlived their savings, through which Dan would nod compassionately. Even if their response is as simple as "How do you do that?" he now has a full invitation to talk about his work and why he chooses to work with MegaFinancial over some of the other firms out there, without coming off as pushy.

Tell me *that's* not a formula for success! People give him *their* cards and ask him to call them!

Because my business is so varied (teambuilding, keynote speaking, coaching, in-class training, writing…), I confess that I don't have one elevator speech anymore. Instead, I do the best I can to guess which aspect of my career would intrigue this person most and hope to get it right. This is part of why I almost always try to ask the other person about *their* career first. The more I know about them, better able I am to focus on an aspect of my business that could be a fit for them, in hopes they will ask me for more information or, better still, my card.

That being said, here's one that I use a lot and it often gets a real dialogue going (sometimes leading me to where the fit might be):

"I create interactive programs for businesses and other organizations using the power of improvisation. It's a lot of fun and I help them work better together and be more successful."

Then I wait and hope they say, "Really? How do you do that?"

By the way, just because someone asks what you do for a living doesn't mean that's what you have to talk about. You can politely answer the question AND change the topic all at once with an answer like this:

"My day job is fastening widgets to gizmos, but my real passion is speaking to groups about how to move past the fear of failure to achieve the great things we are all capable of."

Do you think for a moment they are going to go back and ask you about the widgets after you wow them with that? And every now and then, one of them will say, "Would you come speak to my Rotary/Kiwanis/Religious /Optimists/Women's/Lions club about that?"

By the way, if that speech sounded interesting, you can learn more about *"You Gotta Fail...To Succeed!"* on my website.

---

10.   Listen to yourself speak on tape.

Years ago, I met a woman I'll call "Dorothy". She had a lot of interesting things to say on the topic she was knowledgeable about. Her passion was strong. Her organization skills were good. Her research was thorough.

But Dorothy's voice, at *best*, was drab.

Not only was it nasal, belabored, and whiny, but she also had a loud, sharp laugh that would catch you off guard. It would repeatedly make you jump after your being lulled by the speaking voice. Oh, and Dorothy had a habit of randomly finding amusement in something she had just said, so you never knew when that laugh was coming.

I confess, it actually became kind of fun to watch the uninitiated jump at that laugh and try to hide their reaction.

Unfortunately, for a long time, no one I knew had ever been in a position to give her any sort of advice because she'd never sought any.

One day, I was talking with Dorothy and "Jeremy". Jeremy found a clever way to work into the conversation that he had a program to deliver and that he had *audio taped* one of his rehearsals. "I wanted to get a better idea how I sound from outside my body," he said. "It was very illuminating. Have you ever tried that, Milo?"

I told him that I hadn't done it for rehearsals, but that I'd played back both audio and video of myself *giving* speeches and it had been a learning experience.

"How about you, Dorothy? Have you ever tried that?"

"No," she replied. "But maybe I will."

"Oh, yes, I recommend it highly," Jeremy went on. "I noticed things about how I end my sentences and where I breathe that I didn't realize I was doing."

Later, I asked Jeremy why he brought that up.

"I did learn a lot from hearing myself played back," he replied, "but I brought it up because I thought Dorothy really *needs* to hear what she sounds like if she wants to speak to groups regularly."

I've never known for sure if she took his advice, but I did hear later that she sought out coaching on her speaking skills and I can't imagine that a good coach wouldn't work on her voice technique.

Note: This is different advice than "videotape yourself," of which I'll address pros and cons later. But you can only benefit from hearing yourself played back.

So now you've learned about ten ideas you can work on before you even have a speech to give. That wasn't painful, right? Nobody passed out? Cool. Then you're ready to look at things we can do to get ready for a specific event.

2

10 Sensible Things To Do To Be Ready For A Specific Event

As those in many other professions do, professional speakers love to get together at the National Speakers Association events and swap horror stories of things that have gone wrong. From microphone issues to airport problems to frantic event planners, every time we think we've heard it all, we hear another one.

The majority of those stories, though, come from lessons we've learned along the way - and usually at the beginning. A lot of those mistakes could have been avoided, though, if someone had given *us* a chapter like the one you're about to read, so we'd have headed off blunders *before* they could have happened.

Whether you'll be speaking to large crowds of strangers or to a small group of peers, having a checklist with ideas from this chapter could save you a memorable horror story later.

---

1.   **Find out what manner of dress the *audience* will be in**

Once upon a time, the assumption that you should be dressed to the nines to speak to a group made sense. Every man, from the CEO to the mailroom clerk, was wearing a tie. For women, nothing short of a business suit or an appropriate dress was acceptable.

It's a new century. The old concept of "Dress your best" has been replaced with what I call "Dress to your best advantage."

There are a few factors in determining what your best advantage is. The simplest is to pose the question, "How is the audience likely to be dressed?" When I hear (and I have), "Mostly in shorts and T-shirts...maybe some in jeans...", I don't even consider the suited-up option. Why? Because, as a keynote speaker, one of my goals is to create a sense of rapport with an audience. Dressing like I'm completely different from them adds to the feeling of "otherness" that I'm hoping to eliminate in my time with them. Appearing to be compatible with the group helps my message resonate with them.

Years ago, I met "Earl" at a business function. Earl proudly told a small group of us that he'd recently worn a full business suit to his company picnic because he heard that the CEO would be attending. When one of the men asked me why he'd do that, Earl said with a smile, "I wanted him to see how professional I am and that I would always be the kind of man he could envision representing the company well."

After he left, one of the men in the circle whispered, "Can you imagine what the CEO must have thought of an employee who would so misread a situation? I'd *never* trust him to make a client feel comfortable or count on him to figure out what is appropriate." I have to admit, my instant image was the CEO, probably in a polo shirt and Dockers, *trying* himself to look like one of the "regular folk", looking at Earl in total bewilderment.

A good rule of thumb is to always dress *slightly* better than the audience is expected to. If the audience is to be in a T-Shirt and shorts, the polo shirt and Dockers look might be a good clean look (female equivalent: a simple, pretty blouse with business casual slacks). If the audience is going to be business casual, think nicer business casual or perhaps the tie without the suit jacket. And if your audience is likely to be in ties, you'd need a pretty good reason *not* to look just as formal.

That being said, there are reasons to break the rules on formality. One professional speaker in the National Speakers Association would never think of wearing anything on her feet but sneakers — even with a business suit. It's become her trademark and she brings it up in the speech.

When I started my business, I wore nothing but business suits (well, I also wore shoes and stuff like that, but you know what I mean). Eventually, though, I was seen on the platform by Liz

Goodgold, the branding expert. She approached me later and said "Milo, the suits have got to go. Your material is about bringing out the creativity, fun, and connectedness between people and you are wearing an outfit that says 'no fun zone'. It's a mixed message."

Dress at least as well as your expected audience, but it's also okay to have something that makes you distinct.

With that, she and I discussed other ideas that could not only be more congruent with my message but which also could be a branding item for me. My trademark is now my white suspender braces over bright colors. If you look on my website, you'll find very few pictures of me in a suit. I'm *trying* to project that my programs are colorful, different, and creative because I'm a motivational speaker. And it *has* been helpful to me: I had someone say to me once, "Weren't you in New Orleans last year? I remember those white suspenders!"

If I were speaking on advancing laser technology or crisis management, I would probably not have opted for bright red button-downs with white suspenders. It just happens to work for me because my program is light and because, basically, I work *it*. I'm the "white suspender guy". But even I put on a solid black sports jacket over it when speaking to groups where I suspect there will be more than a few attendees in ties.

2. Get an idea how large the audience will be.

Being heard well is as important as how well you speak. Attendees' minds will wander and their mood will be less congenial if they are struggling to hear.

A good rule, I've found, is that if I'll be speaking more than 10 minutes, I can speak at a confident level to about 75 people in rows or 50 people at tables. Beyond that, I am giving some amount of concentration to being sure that I am projecting fully instead of focusing on my message.

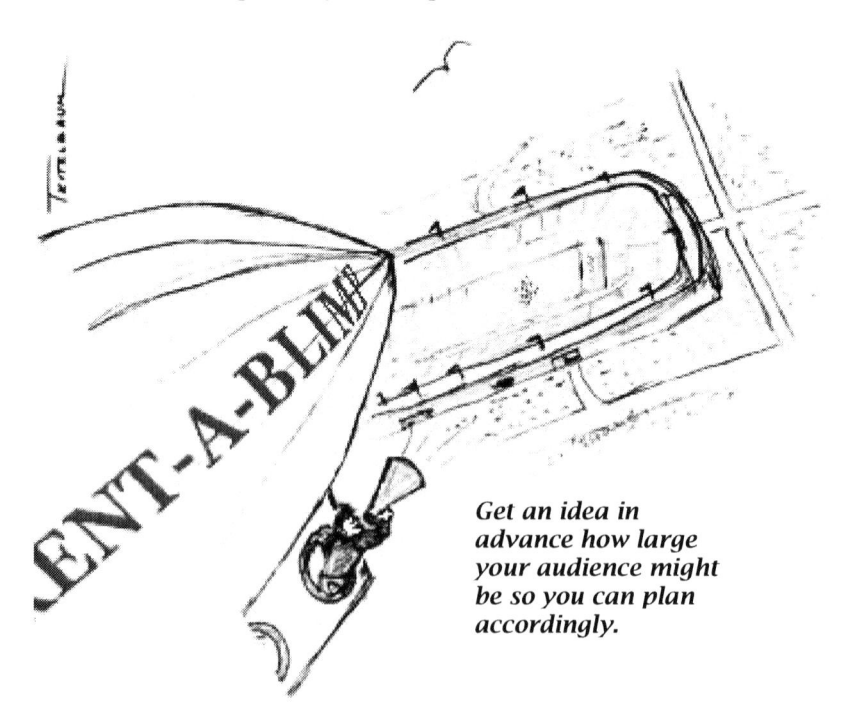

Get an idea in advance how large your audience might be so you can plan accordingly.

The longer you'll be speaking, the more crucial proper amplification will become. Frequently I've heard complaints of not being able to hear a speaker; never have I heard a complaint that amplification was unnecessary. If you have the chance to use it, do! And if the meeting planner says, "Oh you shouldn't need it," remember that they will be judging you afterward, not her.

Recently, a meeting planner told me I shouldn't need amplification. I pressed forward to learn more to see if we were in agreement. She had over 100 people coming to a networking event...with no stage...in a bar...and wanted my program where I lead interactive exercises! How on earth could I have gotten their attention back if they couldn't see or hear me? She agreed to find out about microphones.

With microphones, there are a few options:

Lavaliere

By far, the greatest sense of freedom is when you can turn on a pre-tested lavaliere and simply forget about amplification the whole time you are speaking. There are a few downsides to them that you should be aware of, but aside from that, they are your best amplification tool.

The few things to prepare for are:

1) Arrive early enough to have time to feed the wires beneath your clothing. Otherwise, the swinging leash can be distracting, unprofessional looking, and (worst of all) have the possibility of catching on something as you move.

2) Wear something that can work with the belt clip on the lavaliere. They can fit in a large jacket pocket but then you will feel the base swinging out and back throughout your performance. It is better to have it securely against your body. For men, it clips nicely onto a belt or almost as well on a waistline. For women, the tops of slacks and skirts work fine, but think ahead if a dress is appropriate.

3) Batteries should be brand new or you will discover just how old they are DURING your presentation.

4) Remember that everything you say and do will be amplified. This includes chatting with people doing any exercises you give them, comments you make after you leave the stage area, and (yes, I've heard several tales of this) the trip you make to the bathroom afterward. Use the power-off or mute button any time your voice needs to be localized again.

5) They can be expensive to rent! This might be the simplest factor between getting to use the best possible option and having to accept another form of microphone or deciding to work without any amplification.

Wireless Mikes

These are fine, but if you've not practiced with the loss of one hand, you may be surprised how often you tend to use both!

I have one section of a speech where I portray both people on a phone conversation. Part of how I show that I'm switching between characters is by switching which ear I pretend I'm holding the phone against. When I was given a wireless mike, it didn't occur to me until I was starting the story that I couldn't do it well with a mike in one hand. I now keep the mimed phone on one ear if I have a mike.

While it may feel silly, it might be a good idea to run your program once holding a fake microphone. Anything from your hairbrush to a glue stick to a carrot will work to show you how your presentation feels minus one hand (the Pierre Cardin aftershave bottle is my personal favorite for a microphone shape…and, besides, it's a great scent).

Wired mikes

These are about the same as the wireless in terms of hand usage, but the two handicaps are:

1) You have a limit as to how far you can walk. For most speakers, this is not an issue, but I tend to walk amongst the audience during my interactive sections.
2) You do need to be aware that you are not tangling the cord around anything onstage — including yourself!

Built into the lectern

This is the old school approach that leaves a good speaker trapped behind the lectern and unable to even move much *within* that space.

It should absolutely be your last resort, unless you are still so fearful of speaking that you'd never come out front or if you are so dependent on your notes that you know you simply cannot ever leave the lectern.

None

"None" may sound like an odd choice after all this discussion, but it can be the best option. When I was addressing a group of 25 in a large U-Shape, I opted to pass on a wired microphone because I could step into the "U" a bit and feel certain I'd be heard rather than lose the freedom of one of my hands.

If you go with this option, try to find out in advance if your voice will be well heard, but don't start your speech with, "Can you hear me okay in the back?" You only get one chance to make a first impression and you don't want to waste it on an audio check!

---

3. **Ask what the seating arrangements will be and where you will be in relation.**

In the last chapter, we discussed the pros and cons of each of the set-ups. Knowing the final decision on this may affect how you plan your material.

In addition, your personal height and the height of the podium you will be standing upon (if any) are also factors. They will affect how much of your body will be seen. Albert, who is in the back row behind Tina with the beehive hairdo may be lucky to see you at all. Conversely, Delores in the front row will notice every time you scratch your thigh.

If you plan to make gestures or show props, this could be a factor. If you have to hold a prop over your head for Albert to be able to see it, for instance, that's exactly what you'll need to do!

Obviously, it's best if everyone can see you from at least the waist up. Talk to the meeting planner to find out whether a platform is planned and/or would be helpful.

Remember that a podium is more work for her to arrange, so before you accept her offhanded comment, "Oh, you won't need that," find out for yourself what the situation is, in case she needs to be educated a bit.

---

4. Determine what equipment will be provided vs. what you will have to bring.

This is an area where assumptions can really come back to bite you!

If you do not use PowerPoint, you pretty much only have to discuss audio equipment. If you expect an easel, a flipchart, a whiteboard, markers, or a laser pointer – mention these!. Even if you plan to bring them yourself, bring them up in conversation so effort is not duplicated. You might also discover limitations when you do, such as a tiny platform where an easel wouldn't fit.

If you are partial to overheads, the "overhead projector" and screen need to be arranged. You'll also have to be sure that the overhead projector is going to be accessible to you. Otherwise, you will need to have a designated person to change the plastic sheet for you upon a pre-arranged signal (a nod is best, but it's acceptable to say the person's name if you don't have eye contact).

Be clear on what will be provided and what you will have to bring along yourself.

When PowerPoint is involved there are three key additions to your needs.

The Screen

This is actually the easiest thing to overlook when focusing on the fancy technological stuff. You've gotta shine those slides *onto something*! It's usually easy to find someone to provide one, especially if you're in a professional setting such as a hotel. But it does have to be confirmed!

The Projector

This is a common place where miscommunication can lead to problems. It's important that you make it clear that you are referring to a "computer projector" so that you will not get a slide projector or an overhead projector. I always say "like a Proxima" which is one of the more popular models. Some people only call them Proximas (similar to the use of "Xerox" rather than "photocopier"), so this helps to guarantee that you're on the same page.

Until you're comfortable hooking one up, make it clear that you'll need someone from the group or from a technical department to take care of that.

The Laptop

Unless you are following someone else on stage who is also using PowerPoint, the planner will usually ask *you* to provide the laptop. I caution against this.

Some people have extremely complicated programs that have to integrate with multiple software packages or online services. These people should bring their own laptops so there is no risk of another computer lacking what they need.
For most of us, though, the only software we need is PowerPoint itself. Given that, why worry about configuration issues with your computer? I'll tell you how I put it to the client.

> "I could provide my laptop for the event and I certainly will if that's the only way, but consider this:

"If you provide the laptop (and I'm sure you know a half dozen people attending who could bring one that has PowerPoint on it), you can test the file I'd send you in advance on it and make sure the A/V is working perfectly long before I get there. It's a nice assurance that, when I arrive, we don't even have to *think* about whether there could be any A/V problems while I'm meeting people and getting ready to speak.

"Plus, I'll always bring my laptop anyway as a backup in case you have any problems hooking up yours. If I provide the only laptop, there's no backup."

Nine times out of ten, when I say it like that, they are *eager* to provide the laptop because they see the value in not waiting until I arrive to get things set up.

Having said that, I always send files in advance AND have it on a USB thumb drive AND have it loaded directly on my laptop. I take no chances with the accessibility of my presentation.

If the file is too big to send by email, check out file senders like www.TransferBigFiles.com or any similar tool. There are great free systems out there that allow you to send larger files without attaching them to an email. The recipient gets an email with a link to click on and the download comes afterward. Just search for the words "Send big files" and you'll see lots of options.

---

5. What are the demographics of this audience?

Almost every professional speaker I know has some story about a time they misjudged the demographics of their audience and how they adjusted for it in the future.

One that comes to mind for me was when I spoke to the international conference of the American Society of Training and Development. Because of the word American in there, I forgot to focus on the "international conference" part. And since I was the very first speaker on the first day, I hadn't met any of the attendees yet.

After my speech, which thankfully went well overall, one attendee approached me and said, with a distinct Swedish accent.

"I enjoyed your presentation very much," said Sven, "but I'd like to make two comments. First, for those of us not from America, you talk a bit too fast. I enjoyed what I understood, but I did miss a few parts.

"Second, I'm guessing that this Gloria Steinem that you mentioned is well known in America, but can you tell me who she is?"

The story I told that involved Ms. Steinem could easily have worked with an international audience, but it needed a larger set-up to make it clear to the Svens in the audience who she was.

Other factors to consider, besides nationality:

Age

This can be a big one. Each generation has references that they relate to and, in general, have varying preferences on how they should be approached.

There are also age-related cultural references to consider. While speaking to one man in 2002, whom I estimated to be about thirty, I made a reference to Marlo Thomas. Jordan asked, "Who?" I repeated the name, thinking he hadn't heard me. It never even occurred to me that he wouldn't know who she was.

When he said "Who?" again, I replied, "You know, 'That Girl.'"

He just looked at me oddly and said, "What girl?"

I then realized that this man, who turned out to be 22 at the time, was too young to even have seen *reruns* of the television show, "That Girl". While that made me feel ancient, it was a great wake-up call that references need to be appropriate.

This goes both ways. Your timely reference to the behavior of Mariah Carey at an event might mean nothing to the sixty year old in your audience who still contentedly listens to The Four Tops — on vinyl!

Ethnicity and Culture

While ethnic jokes should almost always be avoided (to be addressed later in the section on humor), ethnic and cultural references can be wisely considered.

Local culture can make a speech seem more personal:

> "Thank you for that lovely luncheon. I haven't enjoyed a meal more since treating myself to the Wacky Burger at Tizzy's Diner." (a well-known local greasy spoon)

Including culturally diverse names makes everyone feel included:

> "Let's say that Lupe calls Jack and Tanisha into his office to discuss an upcoming project…"

Note that this did not have the two women reporting to the man, which would have been noticed by many women in the audience. This brings us to…

Gender

When discussing groups in society, we walk the line between overly broad generalizations and risking ignoring the differences between different segments in society. How do we both "celebrate diversity" and "treat everyone equally"? Very carefully! And gender is certainly one of the distinctions that seems clearest to recognize, if not pin down.

When both men and women can see themselves in books like "Men are from Mars, Women are from Venus", it is worthwhile to appreciate that a Mars audience will react differently than a Venus one. Most of our audiences will be a mix, but the proportion can be a factor.

While I can think of numerous exceptions to everything I can say about gender differences, the following tend to be true and may be worth considering when planning a program, especially if you can find out an approximate male-to-female ratio:

1) Women tend to be more open to and moved by interactive work than men. If there are enough women present,

though, I find that the men are more likely to get into the right spirit for it.

2) Men tend to like stories to be shorter, with more of a "What's the point?" feeling while women tend to get caught up in a well told story and trust that the lesson will come in time.

3) Women tend to be more put off by references that are a bit off-color. While this area should always be walked carefully, the higher percentage of women present, the more likely that you will cross the line with someone.

4) A male audience is going to expect a female speaker to prove herself more. Not fair, just true. Fortunately, conversely, they'll tend to give great respect to the woman who has really proven she deserved to be up there.

English as a Second Language (ESL)

In today's audiences, there is a higher percentage than ever of bright, talented people who did not start out speaking English. It can and should affect your decisions regarding word choice, vocabulary level, idioms, and speaking speed. For example, you might know just what you mean by "beating around the bush", but for an English learner, that doesn't translate well at all!

Work Position

There are situations where it may be beneficial to word something differently when addressing management vs. entry level vs. someone in a position to buy from you. Each of these groups has different motivations.

---

6. **Find out what you can about this group.**

Doing your homework can make a huge difference. I've heard it said that if you customize 10% of the speech, it will feel 100% customized.

Can you review the website of the organization to which you'll be speaking in order to learn organizational goals, key people, recent successes and challenges, and vision statements?

Can you talk to the meeting planner to find out what the greater goal for this meeting is? Are they looking for motivation? To fix a problem? To show appreciation? To plan for changes coming? Knowing this can give you a chance to bend something you'll say to put it in alignment with the bigger picture.

If there is a manager involved beyond the meeting planner, can you get her ear briefly to find out what she's expecting her people to gain from the experience? Or ask her for examples from their environment that support the points you are making.

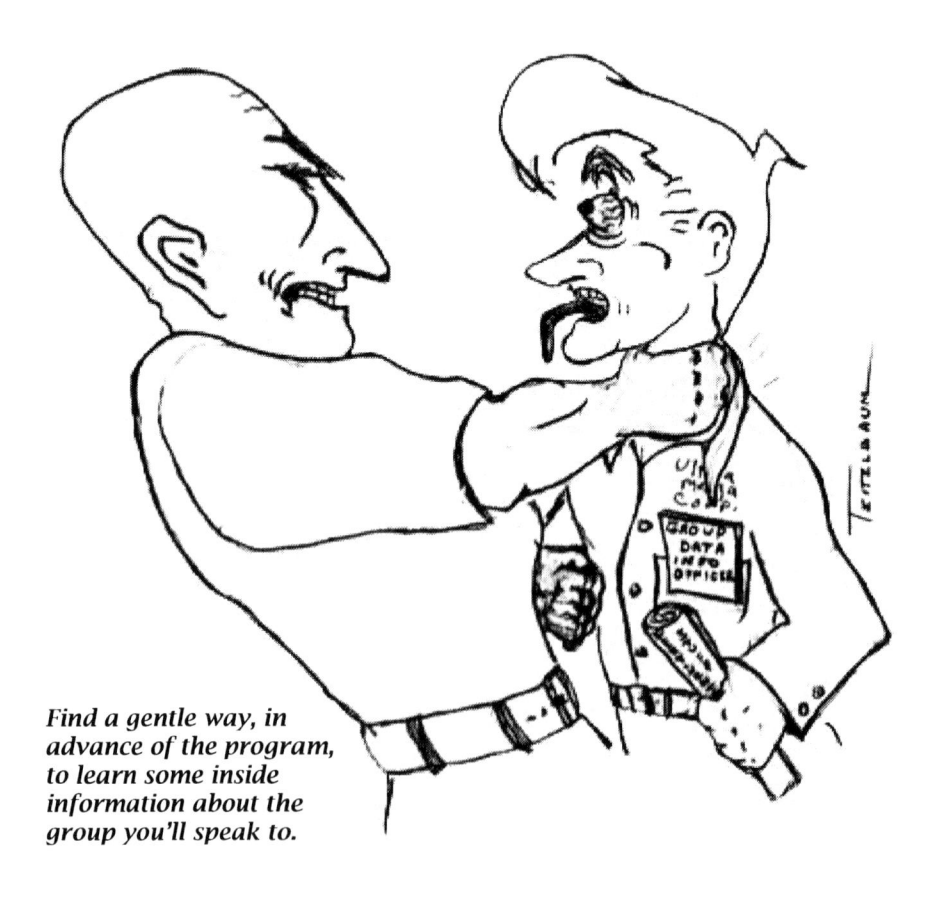

Find a gentle way, in advance of the program, to learn some inside information about the group you'll speak to.

7. **Learn who, if anyone, will precede you on stage. And if someone will...how will you handle the equipment switchover?**

A lot of speakers purposely attend the session right before them because it is empowering. It can only make you look good.

If your topic is "Risk Taking" and the speaker before you is Mel Sharp from accounting, you come across looking like a well-integrated part of the organization when you say:

> "It's important that we be open to taking chances as we move forward together. When Mel was talking about the changes to come in the accounting area, I heard some understandable groans.
>
> But this is far from the first time that we've gone through changes in that area. Is there anyone here who would want to go back to submitting reports in pencil? No? Anyone here who would give up the daily status reports that accounting can now provide because of the automated methods that are now in place? These coming changes may take some getting used to, but let's focus on the benefits!"

Wow! From just *listening* to Mel, you now come across like an integrated part of management. But all you're doing is echoing and building upon it with your material and point of view. But, to the audience, it looks brilliant and premeditated.

---

8. **Are there any hot topics or, conversely, taboo topics right now for this group?**

If you can work in a topic that's on everyone's mind these days or from today's paper, you make it more current and applicable to everyone.

Conversely, you can avoid a world of pain if you find out which topics are taboo or uncomfortable for the group.

I asked this question recently to a planner for an event for supervisors and managers throughout L.A. county. She said,

"Well, I can't think of anything taboo at the moment, but you can avoid alienating a lot of people if you don't treat us all like we're from the *city* of L.A. This is a large county and some of our people live and work in areas that are nothing like the big city."

To be honest, I'm almost sure I *would* have made that mistake if I hadn't asked the question.

This question can let you in on some of the sensitive areas and help you avoid losing your audience. Imagine if you choose an inspirational story about facing your fears by parachuting only days after the CEO's son were hurt in a parachuting accident!

---

9.   How much time will you *really* have?

If they say an hour, you get to talk for an hour. Right? Don't count on it!

I was asked once if our duo could do a fifteen minute presentation. I worked my butt off to cut that program down to a mere fifteen minutes because there was someone in that audience I wanted to impress. It was killing me to slash it that much, but I did it.

Then our introducer started ad-libbing on our intro and ate up *five* of our fifteen minutes! On the fly, without being able to discuss it with each other, we had to cut an additional 30% of our material.

The result? We did fairly well, but felt rushed and completely lost our big conclusion. Had I known that the fifteen minutes would include such an introduction, I'd have planned differently.

Another factor is Q&A. Is this included in your time or after? Is it expected or optional? Do you even want to do it?

Are they suddenly going to ask you for your last five minutes to "take care of group business"? You'd better know up front!

---

10. Will there be a lectern?

If you need one, don't assume it will be there. Ask!

If it cannot be, find out what can be improvised. I've made do with a small table on occasion.

Now that we've looked at key steps to preparing for a speaking event, let's take a look at one way we might cause our audience to lose focus while we're talking to them.

3

10 Things You Can Wear To Distract or Annoy an Audience

Having seen "The Devil Wears Prada", I never want to get "the look" from a Meryl Streep-like client who is giving energy to disapproving my outfit and, in the process, missing my message. Remember that your *message* is the reason for being there and, unless you are wearing something *related* to your message, your outfit should do no more than make a good first impression and then be forgotten.

Let's look at some clothing and style choices that can work against you. (Remember: Based on the chapter title, this section gives you ideas on what NOT to do!)

1. **Wear your cell phone.**

Sure. Let everyone in the place have the feeling that you have more important places to be than with them. While you're at it, leave it on in case someone wants to reach you...

---

2. **Dress less formally than the audience.**

As mentioned earlier, if your audience is in suits, you can undermine your credibility in a hurry by showing up looking "business casual". It looks less successful and implies that you didn't take them as seriously as they take themselves. I repeat this here because it serves not only as an initial poor impression, but as an ongoing distraction.

---

3. **Wear either solid brown, solid black, or orange.**

These colors have been shown in studies to be turn-offs to audiences. Given the many other options, just don't go there. If your only suit is black, consider a bright crew neck in place of a shirt and tie. Or, if that's too informal, go for a yellow or pink shirt to soften the mortician look.

---

4. **Go untucked! It's in style!**

It's the right choice for some nightclubs, but not for most presentations. Unless you're speaking to the fashion industry and *really* know what you're doing, untucked = disheveled...and unprepared for most adults in the business world.

---

5. **Dangly earrings.**

The problem with these is two-fold. On a practical level, they move when you move your head...and you *want* to move your head if you're being animated. So while looking at your face, moving earrings distract an audience from your message.

Second, in the "like it or not" category, there will be some attendees (especially in older crowds) who will see them as less professional looking, possibly even gaudy. Don't give these folks a chance to judge you on anything that beyond your message and your ability to look professional.

And guys, 21st century or not, it's a risk to wear any earrings and hope to be taken as seriously. This is coming from someone who puts his own earring back in the box any time he's speaking.

---

6. The nails.

Sorry, ladies, but anything more than a manicure and a simple clear or one-color polish is both a distraction and potential cause for judgment. Leave the two-tones, glitter, embedded jewels and the like to those who can risk not being taken as seriously.

The same applies for nail length. An able female speaker announced to her audience that she'd be happy to answer more questions on the topic by email. The woman sitting next to me leaned closer and said, "She can type with those nails?" Catty as that may seem, the bottom line was that, on some level, the speaker's nails had captured more of my table companion's attention than her message.

For guys, simplicity is the key. The goal is to have your nails as unnoticeable as possible. That means short, clean, and totally forgettable.

If you're the metrosexual manicure type, hey, that's up to you; nothing wrong with taking care of your cuticles, I guess. But pass on the nail-buffing shine that could have the women (and other men) wondering if you're wearing clean nail polish.

---

7. Women: Really high heels.

The positive feedback you receive elsewhere is not a factor. It's a question of whether you want to allow for the possibility of distraction. Men are not fully taking in your message if they are giving any thought to your legs (side note: at least some of them ARE – even if you don't think so!)

Conversely, some of the ladies in your audience could be investing energy into being holier-than-thou as they wonder, "Who does she think she is, anyway?"

Even if you don't think anyone would care about your tired ol' legs that have never been your favorite feature, high heels will bring attention to them.

If you like them because you feel you need the extra height (listen up, gents), invest in a very simple pair of brown or black boots that can give you about the same height. Mine get me all the way up to 5'6" and give me a chance to make a joke about that fact.

Other shoe "Don'ts" for both genders: sandals, flip-flops (that's "thongs" to you east-coasters), clogs, and sneakers.

So what's a gal to do? Your best bet is a simple low-heeled pair of pumps that are comfortable enough to walk in all day if need be. Flats are fine, too, if they are dressy enough and work with your outfit; just make sure they aren't TOO casual.

Guys? A basic loafer or suede shoe is always good choice. As we'll often wear clothes to shreds (like that 1982 Pink Floyd concert tour T-shirt in your chest of drawers), take notice of whether they've lived a good long life and deserve a proper funeral. If they're still holding up, keep 'em clean and shined.

---

8.   Women: Makeup: Cake it on!

In my first Toastmasters group, there was a woman who I think was probably quite attractive. She was bright, articulate, and probably interesting. Ten years later, all I can remember about her is her lips. She was the Lipstick Lady. Bright, thick, maraschino-red lipstick against the subtle paleness of the rest of her regimen of make-up.

Rarely did she get through a meeting without reaching into her purse to apply another layer, just to make sure it was perfect. It was perfect all right — perfectly distracting.

Less is more when it comes to makeup. Your message is the priority; not you personally. Better to risk looking *less* glamorous than to risk some in the audience thinking you were *trying* to look glamorous!

---

9. Bling!

If you would set off a metal detector, you're probably overdoing it for a speaker. Same deal: those who like it can be distracted by it; those who don't may let it interfere with their opinion.

Rings

Men should max out at one ring per hand; women can push it to a third ring if they must. As we get better at gesturing appropriately with our hands during our presentations, our audience should be caught up in the images we are creating in our minds, not the flash of gold or gems that go with such gestures.

Earrings

For women, two simple earrings that go well with your outfit are best. This classic look usually looks more professional than no earrings at all, although that option is certainly acceptable, too. An additional stud on one side is so common nowadays as to not be given much thought in most cosmopolitan North American settings.

Men should avoid them at best, common as they are in most cities now; if you refuse to give in on this point, choose a small hoop. One exception: youth audiences are so unlikely to have any negative reaction to an earring that it's probably fine to leave any simple earring in place.

Other piercings

21st Century or not, there is no piercing other than the ear that would not evoke an unprofessional image. Even those subtle side-of-the-nose piercings that have gained popularity can be distracting and give the impression that you are too "pop" to be taken seriously.

Necklaces

Men should wear necklines that would hide almost any necklace. Men's necklaces should never be worn on the outside of clothing; many consider this gauche. If it's high enough to be seen, it should be very subtle and against the skin.

Women can get away with more, but remember that every bit of jewelry you add is one more thing that can distract your audience from the reason you are there - to *listen* to you.

Unless you are speaking to a religious group who is of your persuasion, religious symbols should *always* be tucked away. This is hard for some to accept because they feel a sense of strength from their faith and the symbols can be reinforcing. In your audience, however, your open endorsement of a specific religious belief system may make them uncomfortably concerned that it will work its way into the material you cover (and they aren't wrong to wonder - I've seen it happen in settings where it was not appropriate).

It's important that you recognize that no one can take your strength of faith away from you, but for the short time that it takes for you to deliver your speeches, you needn't express it to the world.

Tiaras

Not unless you're in line for a throne. And even then, it's iffy!

---

10. Men: Wear short socks that allow your calves to show if you cross your legs.

You've been hitting the gym; show off those buff calves!

Seriously, while super-short sweatsocks for men have become acceptable, dress socks should always be high enough that you can cross your legs at the knee without skin showing from any angle. (Whether or *not* you are speaking!)

Fashion issues are not just for women...

So now we're looking good and have done our homework. We're ready to show up. But what do we do when we get there? Stay tuned – we're now ready to look at our next not-so-technical vocabulary term: "Arrival Stuff".

4

10 Wise Things To Do When You First Arrive (technical term: "Arrival Stuff")

It may seem like I'm jumping ahead to deal with the day of the presentation without even touching upon organizing your material, planning your introductions, and rehearsing your speech.

Relax! I didn't forget how important those are! But the fear around "The Day" can be so overwhelming that I wanted to look at some of the issues of that day *right now*. Once our problem-thirsty minds have had some of their fears quenched about how "The Day" will go, we can do a better job in our organizing, preparing and rehearsing.

So, okay! It's finally here! Today is The Day of the big presentation! (Not really, you're just reading a book...relax... breathe. I'm speaking figuratively.)

You've arrived at your destination and it's easy to be overwhelmed by the people, the location, and all your brain-overloading thoughts. This chapter gives you some guidelines on what you should do when you first arrive to be ready, willing, and able to do your best.

1. Check in with the person you've agreed to deal with and follow her lead about any other check-ins

You think you're nervous? The person running the meeting is rarely the VIP. It's usually some poor soul who is not only counting on you, but making sure a dozen things are taken care of and worried about making several people in the room happy. She'll rarely get credit for what goes right but will hear about anything that wasn't exceptional.

Befriend this person. It's the kind thing to do and she has the power to make you look good, both in the room and afterward.

Ask in advance "With whom should I check in when I arrive?" It may or may not be the person with whom you've been planning your event. You'll take a load off her mind by asking for her right away and saying hello (with a smile) so she knows all is well.

---

2. Put a bottle of room temperature water on or, if possible, inside the lectern

We'll talk more about voice care later, but for now, put simply, it's good to drink room temperature water periodically while you're presenting.

If you count on the beverage table, you'll likely get chilled bottles or, worse yet, the glasses and pitchers of ice water. It's very easy to cap and uncap a bottle while speaking. It's no fun to carefully lift a glass in and out with a risk of spilling…especially if the glass begins to get condensation.

Bring a small, unchilled bottle and put it inside the lectern as a normal course of your set up.

---

3. Check the mike

The earlier you can do this, the better…especially if you are fortunate enough to be able to do it before anyone else arrives.

If the room is mostly empty, use a full sentence to test the volume. "Microphone Test ▯ 1 2 3" is a good one because it's instantly clear what's happening and not that you are trying to get attention.

If the room is too full to speak unobtrusively, I'll generally use a short, gentle throat clear or "Ahem" to test the volume. If you have a room full of chatting people, they'll generally not even notice this. If you need to do it again, wait 15-20 seconds first so it doesn't start catching their attention.

Whenever possible, do your mike test before the audience is present.

If you'll be wearing a lavaliere, you'll want to thread the wire through your clothes rather than have a big leash hanging around your elbow. This is the time to do it...preferably in the rest room! Especially if you don't have much experience with them, it can be tricky to get that wire from the back of your pants or skirt. It may well require untucking in a less than professional way so you'll want a bit of privacy to get it right.

Note to the ladies: if you use a lavaliere, you need a waistline to clip it onto — most dresses won't work!

And men: lavaliere clips are more secure on a belt than on the waistline of your pants. It's only happened to me once, but it's awful to have the lavaliere pack swing out from behind you while you're talking!

---

4. Check equipment technology

To PowerPoint or not to PowerPoint…don't even get me started on that here; there's a chapter on visuals later. But if you ARE using PowerPoint or some other presentation technology, you'll want to test it right away because fixing it is not something you can rush.

Personally, I like to send the presentation by email in advance to the planner and ask that the A/V person have it ready on slide #1 before I arrive. This accomplishes two things: First, I walk in and see my introduction slide and exhale, knowing that all is well in techno-land. And second, as people come in, they are seeing an ad for me as their speaker for the day, which builds a bit of interest. If they don't want to have that slide showing until I speak, I tell them to put a book in front of the lens, but at least I can see on the book that it's working fine.

If you must bring the PowerPoint presentation yourself, see if you can still get them to have everything ready for PowerPoint and then just plug in a USB thumb drive or whatever your file is saved on. The main thing is that you'll know that the projector and computer are working.

If *you* must provide the equipment, get there *much* earlier because this is usually the worst potential obstacle and you'll know you can breathe easy once you see that first slide on the screen

Make sure the computer is *actually* plugged in…not on battery. I once had two techs rebooting the machine during my presentation, trying to figure out what was wrong. Apparently, the plug was resting *on top of* the outlet (rather than in it) and we were running off waning battery power.

If you'll be using a remote (and PLEASE DO!), test how far you can walk from it and still get a reaction from the laptop. If the crowd is there already, you should still test it, but do it with the book in front of the lens and with a helper to tell you if the screen changes.

---

5. Check your environment.

Are there tables where vision of you or the screen is blocked? I've moved the lectern (with permission) for this reason and the meeting planner never would have noticed the problem otherwise. If you cannot fix what is blocked, consider what you can do during your program to help everyone see as much as possible.

Will you be casting shadows on your own screen? If they expect you'll stay behind a lectern the whole time, they may have centered the screen. As you step out, you are not only blocking the display but you have words and colors all over your body! I ruined what could have been a good video demo this way — only in playing it back did I see how bad that looked.

Can you see the computer if you need to? I try never to have to turn my back on the audience to see my PowerPoint slides. This is easily accomplished by having the actual computer screen where I can see it ahead of me — like a teleprompter. Occasionally, I'll arrive to find the computer faces the audience or, far worse, is in another part of the room. If there's time, correct this. If not, accept that you'll have to look over your shoulder a lot. But if you intend to see the screen yourself during the presentation, try to mention this up front so it can be done right the first time.

---

6. Deal with handouts up front.

Unless your audience is tiny or you have a strong reason not to want people to see your handouts until a certain moment, it's usually wise to distribute your handouts before people arrive, especially if you have marketing materials in there.

First, it's amazing what we'll read before a program if we're sitting alone and getting a little bored, so your material is the best thing they could be reading, right?

Second, it really derails the flow of your presentation to hand out materials in the middle of your program.

By contrast, if you've got fewer than ten people in attendance, perhaps you don't want to run the risk of them looking at papers when they are supposed to be listening to you. That's a call you'll have to make.

At one conference, there were almost nine rows of empty seats between me and the closest attendees because they'd put out so many more chairs than there were reservations, hoping for walk-ins. Sometimes, you can find out from the event planner if this is the plan. If so, I recommend that you put your handouts at the seats you most *want* them sitting in so they'll go where a handout is. If people think they'll miss the handouts, they are more likely to sit where you put them.

Can you guarantee they won't take your handout back to the back row? No, I'm afraid you can't chastise them for that, but my idea will at least increase your odds of a packed house in the front rows.

---

7. Ask the wait staff if a meal can be saved for you

Let's face it – who wants to pass up a free meal? But there's a lot going on before you speak and you want to be focused on that. Plus, our energy tends to lag on a full stomach and you want to be energized!

If the wait staff can hold your meal, you can enjoy it during the time that the meeting wraps up. If that's too much of a hassle, just ask someone at your table to tell the waiter not to clear it when they bring dessert. It won't be hot, but at least it'll be there. Alternately, have a snack with you, especially if you have special dietary needs.

---

8. Ask where you can tuck any clutter.

Laptop cases, purses, pull carts, and the like can be a nuisance at your seat or a distraction on the stage. There's bound to be someplace out of the way for you to put your traveling gear to appear organized and professional.

If there's no one in particular to ask, there's usually a table with a floor length skirt somewhere that will adequately serve you as a storage area.

---

9. Find out where the restrooms are.

Besides the fact that you'll want to check your appearance, especially if you have to feed a lavaliere wire, I've heard two horror stories of professional speakers realizing that they were going to be ill during a program and making mad dashes for the rest room.

One simply excused herself honestly. The other came up with something clever to get the audience involved in during his absence so they hopefully wouldn't even notice that he'd left. He would have gotten away with it, too...if he'd remembered to turn off his lavaliere! I'll leave what happened next to your imagination...

---

10. Once you've done all of this, ask if there's anything you can do to help.

Odds are, there won't be, but you'll endear yourself to the planner for having asked, showing that you don't see yourself as elitist just because you're the speaker. And if there *is* something you can help with, you're a hero.

You can do all of this, right? "Arrival Stuff" sets the stage, so to speak, so that you're ready to focus on doing your job at your best.

Now that we've taken care of the details, let's take care of YOU so that you can shine.

5

10 Helpful Things To Do In The Time Between Your "Arrival Stuff" and Going Onstage

Unless you encounter technology glitches, "Arrival Stuff" usually goes quickly, leaving you time either to stew in anticipation OR to put this time to good use.

This list includes some Do's and Don'ts for that period of time prior to being called onto the stage.

1. **Find a place to warm up your speaking tools.**

I'm amazed how many people don't think of their bodies and voices as the tools of their speech, every bit as much as their PowerPoint and handouts. What's more important at your performance than...your performance? No singer or dancer would perform without warming up – why should you?

Warm Up Your FACE

"Big Face, Small Face" is a great one that some actors use, but I think it's even more valuable for speakers.

Make your face as big as you possibly can: eyes bulging, eyebrows high, mouth open wide, cheekbones as far up and to the sides as you can. Then, make your faces as small as possible: purse your lips and scrunch up your mouth and cheeks toward your nose while making slits of your eyes. Then go back to big face.

Hold each expression for about five seconds before switching to the other. Do about five sets, back and forth, so that your face is physically comfortable and familiar with being in a demonstrative expression that is interesting to view.

This is one of many exercises that I call *"Extremes"*. Extremes are practicing activities as close to the "10" on the 0-10 scale as you can so that you stretch your comfort zone. In this case, the extreme you are working on is the biggest, most inviting, most interesting face you can make, which would be a 10 on the scale.

That being said, Heaven forbid that you should ever give a whole speech at a 10! But practicing 10s makes it way easier to be comfortable with making bigger choices. If we're most comfortable at a 3, it's hard to be comfortable playing at a 6 for a minute, even if that might make your speech more interesting. But if you warm up with 10s, it's much easier to go back up to the 6 on stage.

Another good one I have created is called *"The Chew"*. Start out by chewing an imaginary piece of gum. Then use your face muscles and tongue to keep moving the "gum" into every conceivable part of your mouth including the roof, the top of the throat, behind the lips, along the edges of every tooth (don't worry, it's sugarless and there's no way to choke on it). As you're moving it around, keep chewing it and let your face move as much as possible while you do.

After you've moved it everywhere in your mouth, it magically doubles in size and keeps growing as you keep moving and chewing it, until you can barely keep it in your mouth. The whole Chew exercise can be done in under a minute.

It DOES make a difference to warm up your face. After a presentation series where I was one of ten speakers, a coach approached me afterward and said, "You did face warm-ups, didn't you?" I was surprised and asked how she knew. She said, "You were the only one whose face looked alive up there."

A final exercise that I like and recommend is to *"Smile Five Different Ways"*, preferably in a mirror. They can be genuine, goofy, or a mixture. Then repeat the five smile several times, a little faster each time. It's silly, which should help you relax, but it also increases the odds that you WILL smile naturally during your presentation, making you look warmer.

Facial warm-ups like "The Chew" can make your face look more animated and interesting to watch.

Warm Up Your VOICE

It's not just a phrase. Like a runner's calves, there needs to be some elasticity and movement in the vocal chords before using them effectively for an hour or more. It avoids strain, stumbling, throat clearing, and monotone when we warm up the chords.

"Consonant/Vowel Blends" is an exercise I do in the car on the way to every speech, but I'll repeat it if I get time alone before a speech.

Make the sound of every consonant, followed by each of the long vowels:

Bay Bee Bye Boh Boo.
Cay Key Kye Coh Coo.   (use the K sound)
Day Dee Dye Doe Doo.
(and so on.)

When you're done (and you'll get very quick at it with practice), repeat this with the short vowels. You can add a final "d" to the sound if that's easier. To help you know what sounds I mean, I've included that "d" below, but it's not necessary:

Bad Bed Bid Bod Bud.
Cad Ked Kid Cod Cud.
Dad Ded Did Dod Dud.
(and so on.)

The great value in this is that, once you've run the long and short vowels through, you've made almost every sound you are likely to in your speech. It's familiar to your mind and body now so you're less likely to trip up when it counts.

Tongue Twisters are a great way to get your brain and mouth in gear. The alliteration (words starting with the same sound) of a word here and there will feel like nothing after the effort of the tongue twisters. Don't worry if you struggle with them; they're supposed to be hard. It's not about *succeeding* at them; it's about putting your brain through the exercise. Having done them, nothing you say on stage is likely to be nearly as difficult as a tongue twister, so your mouth and mind will be in top shape!

Here is the list of the ones that I warm up with to ensure I hit each of the consonants and several of the blended sounds:

Betty Babble Bought A Big Blue Basket.
Carla Can Come Cause Caberet's Closed Captioned.
David Dipped the Dunking Donut.
Funny how Fergy Fell on her Fanny.
God Goes Ga-Ga for Gospel and Go-Go.
He has hope he'll have his holiday.
Jenny chews gingerly since jamming her jaw.
Kenny Killed the Clunky Cat.
Let's Let Lisa Looking Longingly Along The Lanai.

Momentous moments make me mix my metaphors.
Never nab a nanny's noodles.
Poppa puts pepper and paprika on popcorn.
Quentin quietly quivers and quakes.
Rapid rabbits rarely race real railroads.
On **S**unday, Selma saw Sally sifting salt.
Try to tell Tony to tootle Tom's trumpet.
Vicki vacuumed with vigor and vim.
Wally was wise when watching Wanda's wombat.
Young youths used to use yummy yogurt.
The **Z**oo's zealous zebra zig-zigs like Zeus.
She sure shakes sugar.
Three thousand thin thrushes thrive thriftfully.
The **Ch**illy child cheats at Chinese Checkers.

Warm Up Your Body

Your body? Who cares about your body when you're there to speak? You do!...for two reasons. One, quite simply, is that your body is attached to your head (or it certainly should be). If your body is tense, it'll affect your mind and face more than you may realize.

The other reason is that you *should* be using your body more than you think. I'm not expecting you to look like a sign language interpreter, but we will talk, in a later chapter, about using your body more. So let's warm it up!

Head rolls are a simple yet effective way to release tension and you can even do them in front of people. One key to doing them right is to ignore the terrible directions you may have been given way back in your high school Phys Ed class or in the cool down at some Aerobics Studio. Read on...

Start by putting your chin to your chest and looking down, as if looking at the 6 o'clock position on a clock. Then slowly roll your head to the left, extending your ear as close as you can get it to your shoulder until your chin is pointing to the one-o'clock position. *Do not take it all the way* to the 12-o'clock position, which crushes those poor little bones and *creates* tension! Hold it at 1 o'clock for about two seconds, then reverse the roll, passing the initial 6 o'clock point and stopping at the 11 o'clock position. Go back and forth slowly like that, never completing the circle.

Limb circles are great if you can get a moment alone. For the legs, put all of your weight on your left foot. Then lift the right foot and circle the ankle clockwise. Add circling the knee while keeping that ankle going. Then add the hip joint so all three are going. Now touch the foot down for a balance rest. Repeat by circling the body parts counter-clockwise. Then repeat both phases with the other leg.

It takes a bit of coordination, so do it as fully or as simply as you can without risking falling over.

For the upper body, you'll do the same thing, but instead of doing ankle-knee-hip, you'll do wrist-elbow-shoulder. And if you're coordinated enough, you'll find you can do both arms at once. (I don't recommend this for the legs because I'm yet to meet someone who can rotate both hips at once while standing!)

The fact that it takes a little concentration to coordinate this is a good thing. Not only will it loosen up your body, but you can't really focus on fear while trying to coordinate these, so your body is forced to let go of that part of its tension.

Believe it or not, you can get away with doing leg circles in the restroom. If the door opens, it only takes half a second to put your foot down so no one will know what you were doing! And I've done arm circles so subtly that people couldn't tell I was doing them at my table. Feel free to have fun with it!

---

2. **Run your opening in a private place where you won't be heard.**

Most of us relax a little when we've gotten through our opening. Generally, it's the part we've memorized or at least outlined more intensely.

Go ahead and just run through those first few minutes. You can do them at normal speed or you can do a speed-read without emotion and inflection. I like doing the latter to convince myself I REALLY have it down and then go back and do it again at a comfortable pace, so I remember not to rush.

A clever way to do this without feeling awkward is to find a semi-private space or go outdoors and do the whole thing into your cell phone. You won't look crazy and no one will know!

Find a private place to run your opening.

---

3.   **Go back and meet people.**

Attendees are more interested to listen to people they already like. Mill about and introduce yourself. That way, you're less of a stranger when you come to the stage.

I like to have a couple of places in my speech where I can reference specific examples from the group. If there's time, I'll ask a few people whom I met earlier if they can provide me with a few of these examples.

They usually enjoy being able to talk about their organization (because usually no one outside really cares that much) and they get a kick out of hearing me bring up their idea on the podium. But the main thing it accomplishes is creating rapport with some of the attendees before going up there. And they may even talk to their cohorts about the conversation, giving you more allies.

---

4. Avoid (or at least pace) your caffeine.

What — speaking in front of a whole group of people isn't nerve-wracking enough without making yourself *jittery*, too?

You're likely to have enough adrenaline going - you don't really need caffeine, too. As we get nervous, we tend to pick up our pace where, the truth is, most of us need to actually be pacing ourselves more precisely.

If you're dead to the world without your caffeine, then drink the minimum you'll need, but don't try to pump yourself up so you'll be "better" or "livelier".

---

5. Breathe!

I'm not being facetious. When I coach people on their speaking, it's clear that breathing is one of the first things to go when stress kicks in. It's a vicious cycle: when your body notices that you aren't breathing, it generates additional stress. Trick your body into thinking you are calm and it'll start to happen.

A great exercise that you can do (even with others around you) is *Breath Count*. Imagine yourself in front of the room and everyone looking to you with smiles and nods. Take as deep a breath as you can and then let it out as slowly as you can (the latter is the harder part). Count as you exhale. Repeat until the long exhale count gets to a number you feel good about and isn't as challenging anymore.

Just see if you don't feel better about the whole experience afterward — even if you weren't nervous at all, it's a nice calming feeling. And it's hard to focus on anything else when you're working on adding yet one more number to your count, thus breaking the fear cycle.

---

6. Listen to what's happening in the meeting.

While the meeting topic and acknowledgements might seem dull to an outsider (trends in the world of concrete thickening may not be what floats your boat, for example), they can also be a wealth of information from which you can ad-lib.

In your examples, reference names and facts you heard them say. If the president thanks Mary Carlson for all her hard work on the Christmas party at the Hilton, think how you can use that. If your topic is sales, mention how many ways Mary must have been subjected to sales techniques in pulling off that great party. If your topic is "Branding", talk about what images came to mind when you first heard that the Christmas party was going to be at the Hilton. And so on.

Let's say, as per my example, there is a new way of thickening concrete faster. You could use that if you had a section on adapting to change, staying current with technology, managing new processes, and many other topics.

It might seem silly, but it goes a long way in making you seem like one of the gang...and that develops rapport!

---

7. Stay hydrated with the right choices.

Dry mouth can be distracting to you and to your audience (I critiqued one tape where I had to point out to the speaker how many times he licked his lips – it was almost nonstop!) Stay hydrated to avoid discomfort and to protect your voice.

We've already talked about avoiding caffeine, but there are other issues with drinking to mention:

- Alcohol – Not until after you're done! I've accepted a drink (even taken a sip out of politeness), but then it sits at my table until I'm done. Don't give in to the idea that it'll "take the edge off". Use other methods to relax.
- Juice – Remember that your vocal chords are your tool and the goal is to lubricate them. Juice is wet, but it's also sticky, which can undermine your goal. The same holds true for

honey, jelly, and syrup. (Yes, I know that nobody *drinks* these – but you get my point)

- Soda — Only you can decide if you'll be able to go the whole length of your program without the carbonation coming back on you. Personally, I don't risk it!

Hydrate yourself... appropriately!

- Milk — The creamy nature of milk products makes them phlegm producers, increasing the odds that you'll want to clear your throat more than normal.

Am I leaving you anything? Well, my top recommendation is room temperature water. If you'd like something with a soothing feeling, herbal teas (but not mint ones) are good choices, especially the one made by Traditional Medicines called "Throat Coat". It is designed to soothe without masking symptoms. Decaf and regular tea are usually fine as well so long as they are not *too* hot. Scalding your chords is the only thing worse than freezing them.

---

8.   Eat lightly, if at all.

Studies have shown that one of the worst times for an audience to be attentive is right after a meal. Their brains go to relaxation and digestion instead of thinking. And 90% of the time, you'll be asked to be the "after lunch" or "after dinner" speaker, starting you off with a strike against you.

As you cannot change how the client schedules you, there's no way to improve the audience's condition of fullness. But you CAN change your own energy level to account for it and one of the key ways is not to put *yourself* in the same gentle stupor!

As many meetings put a meal in front of you, it's tempting to want to take advantage of it. If possible, opt to eat it colder afterward rather than while it's hot beforehand. It may not be as tasty cold, but clearly the speech is the more important factor. (Sometimes, I'll ask the waiter if a hot meal can be saved for me afterward and usually, if they know you're the speaker, they'll do it.)

If there is no meal provided, my rule tends to be:

"Eat a light breakfast before a morning program;
 Eat a big breakfast to hold me through a lunchtime speech;
 Eat a big lunch to hold me through a dinner speech."

9.   **Recheck that your cell phone will not ring and make sure it's not on your body at all.**

Thin as they are getting, cell phones (like keys, pens, wallets, etc.) should not be in front pockets, looking bulky and unflattering. Likewise, phones clipped on the waistline look somewhat tacky when addressing a crowd. Find a good place to leave your *turned-off* phone.

That being said, forgetting to turn off your phone is embarrassing enough when it's on your hip, but when it's halfway across the room because you didn't keep it on you, that's mortifying (and yes, it happened to me with a new phone that I silenced incorrectly). So be very sure of the ringer status before setting it aside.

Even a vibrate mode can be distracting. I once watched a speaker's phone vibrate across and off a table! It drew everyone's attention in the area. During your speech, opt for "OFF".

---

10.   **Check your fly.**

It really can't hurt. And boy, can it help! I remember a lecture on statistics where no one could focus on anything but the speaker's bright-white boxers; they were like a mental bull's-eye against his solid black pants!

Tip for the gents: through the fly is the best way to tuck in your shirt; just give a tug on the tails from the inside and zip back up...but only if you can find someplace private to do this!

Okay, now you are ready to go onstage. But is the audience ready for *you*? A well-done introduction can make the difference between the audience eagerly anticipating your first few words or losing interest even before you start.

Let's look at the introduction now.

6

10 Survival Tips Regarding Introductions

Hey, you're the speaker; the introduction is someone *else's* job. All you can do is hope they do a good job, right?

Not if you're a wise speaker who uses your experience to set *yourself* up well! There's a lot you can do to make sure that the introduction works *for* you — even though you won't be delivering it yourself.

1. **Never EVER let the people you'll be addressing create your introduction.**

This is essentially the biggest mistake I see speakers make regarding introductions. Who knows better than you how you should be introduced? Do you expect them to take pain-staking time to research your website to do a great job? Or even to review a bio you provided to figure out what parts are best to mention?

I am yet to encounter a group where they aren't happy to read what you give them. This does not mean that the introducer can't warm up the crowd, do greetings, tell a joke, etc. It means that all of that chatter which you don't control *precedes* the actual introduction for you. This prevents any distracting tangents once your primary intro has begun.

Early in my career, I had a mere *fifteen* minute timeslot to speak at a convention. There was someone in the audience that I *really* wanted to impress. I planned a very tight 14 minutes, counting on about a one minute introduction. Instead, the woman went on and on about how much she liked me and how much fun my work is. That's great and very sweet, but I ended up with only nine-and-a-half minutes to speak, forcing me to rush through parts in order to finish on time.

If I'd given her a script, I would have been significantly better off.

Create your own introduction to give the introducer, rather than hoping you'll like the one that he comes up with for you.

2.   If you know someone there who you think would read it well, ask for them.

Often, you won't know your introducer or their skills. I've had people who were outstanding and others who just looked like they were miserable up there.

If you know someone there who you think would do a good job, ask that person if she would be willing to be your introducer. If they agree, contact the group and say, "I've known Kathy for a few years and I'd be honored to have her be my introducer, if that'd be okay." Usually, this will be acceptable and you'll feel confident that you're getting someone that you can count on.

3.   Send it to the introducer in advance.

Few of us read something well if we've never seen it before. With email and faxes, there's no reason not to send the appropriate wording to your introducer in advance so she can have an opportunity to familiarize herself with it.

4.   Ask if she would please read it aloud in advance.

What looks good on paper may not be as effective coming across our tongues. My current introduction refers to the humorous author Erma Bombeck. I grew up knowing that name, but introducers often stumble on it quite a bit.

If you make this request in terms of making the *introducer* look good, she shouldn't mind being asked to read it once aloud. Perhaps you might say:

"Kathy, I want you to come across well and I've noticed that my introducers usually look more confident up there if they've read it <u>aloud</u> once or twice before the day of the engagement. Can I ask you to do that?"

5.   Bring a hard copy anyway.

Several times, I've been asked for the hard copy in spite of sending it in advance. And what will you do if the anticipated introducer calls in sick? Bring a hard copy, just to be safe!

---

6.   Include pronunciation guidelines for any "non-dictionary" words that could be mispronounced, like your name.

When 1 in 4 people guess my name as MEE-low instead of MY-low, it doesn't hurt to put the correct answer right on the intro page for them.

Likewise, my company name IMPROVentures is pronounced "Improv Ventures", but people make all kinds of guesses at it, so I give them a guide to that as well.

Look over your intro and see if there's anything in there that might be guessed wrong and provide the right answers in advance.

---

7.   Put a message about turning off cell phones in your printed introduction.

I always put the following sentence in bright red as the *first* line of my printed intro:

> "Please silence your cell phones if you still have them on."

Then I put in parentheses, still in red:

> "(you can skip this line if this has been announced since the last break)."

While it's not considered appropriate for *me* to mention the cell phones, it's totally appropriate from the introducer, especially when it seems like a side note before he starts talking about me. If I don't put it there, he may not say it and I'll be the one stuck dealing with a phone ringing ten minutes later.

A simple mention, scripted into your introduction, is one of the subtler ways to remind people to silence their cell phones.

8. **Find out where you'll be approaching the stage from and make sure the introducer knows, too.**

Sometimes, you'll be coming from the edge of the stage area; sometimes you'll be coming from a seat; sometimes you'll be coming from the back of the room. It usually depends on the stage set up but you and the client may have different ideas.

As you probably know what feels best for you, I recommend approaching it as a request rather than a question:

"May I wait over by that side door during the introduction so that I'm close by but not stealing focus?"

Generally the best place, I find, is a few feet off from the side of the stage, if there is a stage. If there's no stage, be a good ten feet off to her side so she has the audience's full attention.

---

9. **Extend your hand toward the introducer as you get close, making it clear that you *are* going to shake.**

In North America, one of four things is likely to happen as you approach the introducer:

> 1) A handshake
> 2) A kiss on the cheek
> 3) A hug
> 4) No physical contact

Options 2 and 3 may have caused you to chuckle, but both can occur in settings where people have known each other for quite a while (particularly between female friends).

More common, of course, are options 1 and 4. For the introducer who doesn't see it coming, it can be an awkward guessing game, especially if she's picked up objects from the lectern so her hands are full.

I like to mention to the introducer that I will shake her hand and I'll use the walk-with-extended-hand as a reminder. That way, there's no strange little back and forth dance as you try to figure out what's going to happen.

It may seem insignificant, but it's your first exposure to the audience; make it clear and professional.

---

10. **If feasible, use PowerPoint in a manner where *you* control the frame advance during your introduction**

Almost no one does this, but it's highly effective and I get great feedback on it.

While my introduction is being read by someone else, I advance the PowerPoint slides behind her. This adds visual stimulation for the listener and is a great place to add a bit of humor if you can.

For instance, in my own introduction, as the introducer is talking about the various work I've done at different points in my life, I show pictures of myself with humorous comments about my ever-changing hair and facial hair (i.e., "Big hair phase", "Obligatory 2001 Goatee"). It usually gets laughs and immediately draws people into my energy before I ever get to say a word.

Because it's an unusual approach, let the introducer know, in no uncertain terms, that all she has to do is stay on script and you'll take care of the slides.

It also prevents them from adlibbing TOO much, because they know that the slides are sequenced. Not a bad thing at all!

That's all quite manageable, right? But wait! All we've discussed is how to make the introduction successful. We haven't said anything about what the introduction should and shouldn't include! No worries. As luck would have it, we're ready for a Top 10 list on that! What a coincidence!

7

10 Considerations About What Your Introduction Should(n't) Include

A good introduction sets you up do be viewed with respect and anticipation. Let's take a look at a few of the Do's and Don'ts for this important speech feature.

1. **Briefly remind them why you're the person here ...without covering material.**

An effective introduction gives background on your qualifications to be speaking to this group. A good way to do that is to begin with a statement about how your background relates to the topic overall (degrees, work experience, etc.) and then, if applicable, move toward specifics on why you are a fit for this group on this topic.

Unless your topic is so serious that you will use no humor at all, it is not only acceptable but actually wise to see if you can put in something worthy of a chuckle into the intro.

This is probably a good time for me to mention something that even many professional speakers struggle with. Being humorless does not make you look more professional! No matter what your topic is, people want to like you and enjoy the experience of hearing you.

What's funny about my topic for an introduction, you ask? Let's say your name is Doris and you speak on time management. In just one line of your introduction, you can include, "Doris has taught thousands of corporate employees at MegaCorp to be more effective with their time, although she admits that she still can't get her husband Alan to a movie before the previews are over."

You'll get a chuckle, you look more human, and you're ready to roll.

---

2. Distinguish yourself as being separate from the group - at least for a little while.

There's a saying in the speaking industry: "No one thinks you're an expert if you're not from another city." Somehow, it's as if people we know (or even who shop at the same mall as us) couldn't be experts.

So your intro, in part, is to give someone that *they* know a chance to convey the impression, "Hey, this guy has a boatload of experience and we're lucky to have his time for the next hour...so listen up!"

---

3. Provide a connection between the group and your topic.

That being said, it's critical that you're shown to have relevance to the group.

For instance, Doris' attendees all make plastic pacifiers; she doesn't. She speaks on time management; they don't. Where's the connection for them?

The introducer will *make* the connection for everyone when the customized introduction you prepared for her includes, "With the announcement that the ADA is no longer opposed to pacifier usage, we may see higher product and time demand...and we're fortunate to have an expert here to talk about managing our time. Please help me welcome Doris!"

(Who is this Doris and why does she keep showing up in my examples?)

4. **It is NOT about the introducer.**

A history of the connection between you and the introducer is not needed. If there is some *relevant, interesting fact* that makes your relationship worth mentioning, then perhaps you might use it to make you look good, but not to flatter your introducer.

Here's how it can work effectively, if it's used at all:

"When I first met Doris in 1994, she was just beginning to get excited about how her time management programs were benefiting MegaCorp. Now, with her own business, her programs are being used in over a dozen Fortune 500 companies and her ideas are sure to make a difference for us."

Note that the relationship is only used to give you credibility, not to flatter the introducer for knowing you.

5. **Beware of taking an ego bath.**

You can establish credibility and credentials without turning it into an episode of "This Is Your Life!"

Give your background and mention a couple of successes, but don't feel that they have to know *every* great thing about your experience. You just need enough in there to make them think, "Okay, he deserves my attention for a while."

6. **It's okay to include appropriately-connected personal information.**

As in the example above about Doris, it's okay to bring in a little personal info to develop rapport with the audience, even if it's not for humor.

"Doris has to manage her own time very carefully with her own business, three kids, and a board position with her favorite charity, the American Lung Association."

If your intro gets too long, you may want to cut this, but personally, I like hearing a human reference and find that audiences do, too.

Let your introduction explain well what your credentials are...without it becoming an ego bath.

7.   **Remember that not every introducer will know how to use a punch line.**

Humor is rare in our business lives so it's usually appreciated... but keep in mind that you can't count upon your reader having a talent for timing.

If a line needs to be said *just right* to get the laugh, it's better to find a different line.

---

8.   **If the audience needs to be aware of a handout, have the introducer mention it so you don't have to.**

It's a little awkward to be on a roll and *then* notice that people don't realize you're referencing a handout on their table.

To resolve this, have the introducer include something like, "Milo's handout is in fill-in-the-blank format, so you might want to have it in hand."

(Thought I'd give Doris a break – she needs to go deal with that husband who's always late.)

---

9.   **Include the speech title.**

If a title is appropriate for your speech, have the introducer say it towards the end of the introduction to remind people of the theme of your program:

"We're pleased to have him here for a little fun and some valuable thoughts for our newly merged team. With his speech 'You Gotta Fail...To Succeed!', please welcome Milo Shapiro!"

You might think your topic isn't "title worthy". But often it is — just in a less formal way. Consider:

"We've had an interesting year with some real highs and lows. Here to present an outline of the second quarter sales figures is the accounting department's general manager, Jennifer Coburn."

That doesn't sound awkward, does it? But subtly, this manager has set Jennifer up as an expert and created a sense of the title "Outline of the Second Quarter Sales Figures", which creates a reasonable expectation of what is to come.

---

10.   End with your name, possibly saving it until the very end.

Making your name the last thing the introducer says gives you clout and sets up the audience to either begin applause (if appropriate) or at least to give you their full attention.

One technique a lot of speakers employ is to hold off on using their name anywhere in the introduction until the last possible moment, almost like an Oscar award:

"Our speaker today is a graduate of...He has worked in companies as large as...He is the author of...Please welcome Doris Morris!"

It's not a technique I happen to use, but I've seen work effectively.

If you'd like to see an example of one of the more effective introductions I have used in the past, you can see it posted at www.MiloShapiro.com/books/resources. It's a little longer than I would recommend for most people, but I can get away with mine being a *little* longer because of the humorous slides being shown behind the introducer. The visual stimulation and the humor allow it to feel shorter.

All right! You're ready to be introduced! You're ready to walk out on that stage! Are you ready to get through the first ten seconds on stage? A lot can go right or wrong in that little time...let's take a look!

8

10 Great Ways To Blow It In Your First Ten Seconds

We've all heard what they say about first impressions. Well, it's all true. After a rough start, you might have to spend the rest of your time on stage trying to win the audience back. The good news is that a good first impression is just as powerful on the positive side - and some simple pointers can set you up for success.

Just for fun, this chapter is written as more of a **"Don't" List** — things I hope *never* to hear that you've done. Avoid these ten mistakes and you're much more likely to succeed!

1. **Wait for your introducer to leave the stage so you can enter it empty.**

Sure. Leave that stage wide open so the audience can be confused and lose focus.

You're going on the podium, not "The Price Is Right!" Take your time approaching the mike.

2. **Run on stage like "The Price Is Right".**

Throw away your professionalism and capture their attention instead with your manic-ness.

---

3. **Wave down the applause.**

You're so amazing that the polite applause they want to show you is really beneath you. (Note: if it ever *really* does go on an awkward amount of time, simply say "Thank you" every few seconds until it's clear to everyone that you'd like to start and applause will subside naturally.)

4. Comment on the introducer.

Spend your first valuable moments talking about the person who was just on stage instead of capturing their attention with something that will make them want to listen to you for the next hour.

---

5. Start talking before they have completely stopped applauding.

That'll teach them not to stop clapping when you have a lot to say! And those first few missed words will add an air of mystery that your presentation would have been lacking otherwise.

---

6. Bow.

Yes, I've seen it and it looks as silly as it sounds. Perhaps in some other cultures it is appropriate, but in western culture, it looks really odd...especially *before* you've done anything.

---

7. Do a mike check.

An audience is anticipating knowledge, insight, humor, and a dynamic performance from a speaker. So, of course, nothing is more captivating and exciting than to lead off with:

"Can you hear me in the back? Does this sound okay? Is this on?"

Seriously, test it beforehand if you possibly can. Otherwise, assume the best and go right into your opening. In the odd case where your first sentence isn't loud enough, you'll probably notice and you can stop to deal with it...and then start again...with a smile to show you're a good sport about such things happening.

8. Read text from your first slide.

We'll talk more about PowerPoint later, but even if you're going to have a lot of text on there PLEASE don't speak directly from it in the first thirty seconds.

---

9. Say hi to someone you know in the crowd.

"Hey, Tom! So glad you could be with us. Love the new haircut! Doesn't he look great everyone?"

Wonderful. Now Tom is the focus instead of you. And anyone who doesn't know Tom feels like an outsider.

---

10. Start with "Good morning".

It's not a horrible mistake, but it's weak. So are "Hello" and "Thank you."

So many of these points come back to the basic premise: you get one chance to make a first impression. Don't waste (as Emerill the chef would call it) your one chance for a "Bam!"

Throw out a cool fact that'll make 'em go "Hmm!". Launch into an interesting story that you'll create relevance to. Pose a challenging question. Make your first words as interesting...as you are!

Hey, you've gotten through the first ten seconds. *Mazel Tov!* — I'm proud of you! If you can just get through the next *twenty* seconds successfully, you're well on your way. No, we won't analyze your entire speech in tiny increments, but a good start is so important that it warrants more than these ten points. So let's look at your Opening now.

9

10 Bonus Ways To Blow It In Your First *Thirty* Seconds

Don't let the chapter title scare you! By **avoiding** these additional mistakes, you'll be off to a GREAT start!

But if, however, for some odd reason, you really *wanted* to mess up, here are some things that could make you **less** effective.

1. **Thank them, the company, committee, introducer and anyone else who in any small way brought you here.**

Although this is a continuation of the theme "Make a strong first impression", it bears highlighting because it's so commonly done and often goes on well beyond the ten second mark. It's more important to them that you do a good job than prove your appreciation. If you really appreciate them, show them by giving them your best effort.

One of my coaching clients, a successful architect, was invited to give a speech to an audience of architecture enthusiasts. He fought me on this point, saying he HAD to thank them for the honor or he'd look ungrateful. Finally, I said to him, "Let's role play. You be the introducer and I'll be you. Introduce me."

He read the introduction we'd written for him. I shook his hand, mouthing "thank you" to him (as if applause were drowning out my words). He sat down and I began improvising an opening, based on some of the material I knew he'd be talking about:

"Which was a bigger step forward in the history of architecture...the completion of the pyramids or the erection of the Empire State Building? (a pause) Of course, there's no real answer to that, but the significance of the question is recognizing that, in each period in time, new forms were created to meet new needs."

I turned to him then and said, "Did it appear rude that I didn't thank anyone?" He thought about that for a moment and said, "No, I got caught up in what you were saying right away." And that's what your attendees *really* want.

If you are aching over not thanking the group, you can **end** your opening with something along the lines of:

"...In the next thirty minutes, it's my honor and privilege to share with you some of the research that I've been able to do on the history of architecture and how those forms are being incorporated into today's design."

And that's enough with the gratitude... This ain't the Academy Awards!

---

2. **Remind them of who they are.**

"Ladies, Gentlemen, Fellow Stockholders, Staff Members, and Guests..."

Blah. Blah. Blah. They know who they are.

---

3. **Apologize for anything that's not perfect in the room.**

"Let me start by saying that the stage is lower than I expected so if you can't see in the back, I'm really sorry, but I'm sure your committee did the best they could with their budget..." Worse than blah blah blah. That's just awkward and clunky.

If such an acknowledgement is necessary, wait for as long as possible to bring it up so more important matters are said <u>first</u>. In the example above, don't acknowledge the low stage until you have something to show them. Then hold it high and simply say, "I'm holding it as high as I can for those of you in the back. I hope you can see." 'Nuff said!

---

4. Apologize for things they probably don't even know or notice.

"Before we start, I just want to say that I'm sorry about...:

- the coffee stain on my shirt
- the fact that I didn't get here quite as early as I intended
- the fact that the PowerPoint is a little small
- the fact that Mercury is in retrograde and an eclipse is coming soon

People *get* that things go wrong and either they'll account for them or, more often than you think, not even have given them consideration. Let it go.

If there is a pink elephant in the room so enormous that you think it will be a distraction if you don't account for it, see if you can get the *introducer* to take it on so *you* can still start strongly with real material:

"Before I introduce today's speaker, I need to let you know that we are still working on getting his lavaliere working. So if he appears to be stuck behind the lectern in that corner, it's just so that he can use that microphone. As soon as we get that working, he'll be able to come front and center. Moving on, our speaker today is a man who..."

---

5. Tell a disturbing story to make them feel for you as a person.

There's a difference between a self-deprecating story to create a bit of human rapport and turning the platform into a cross between a confessional and a therapy session!

If you have a story that relates strongly to the theme and will empower people in some way, it's okay to get personal and let them into your world. But the audience should leave motivated or educated in some way, not just feeling sorry for you and sharing your anger at something unconnected.

In my customer service presentation, for example, I discuss the sub-par customer service I once received from a health care company. If I left it at that, the impression would be merely, "What a shame that poor man got such a run-around!" Where's the learning in that?

Instead, however, I flip it by transitioning to how *amazing* the last person I dealt with was. He changed my attitude about the company by going so far outside the norm to correct my situation and left me feeling certain that the issue would be avoided in the future. That's a WOW, not a boo-hoo.

---

6. **Talk about what you've done since arriving in their town.**

"Thank you so much. Boy, it's great to be here. I can certainly see why your zoo is so famous. I'm sure glad I came in a day early before speaking so I could make a little time for that. And hasn't this hotel got a great lobby?..."

Unless it's got a great tie-in to your material or it's a *really* endearing story, it has little to do with why you're before them at this moment and just wastes time.

---

7. **Tell a joke someone forwarded to you.**

Do you want to bet on the fact that no one else in the room has the internet? Or that you're the only one who gets jokes forwarded to them?

It's almost painful to hear a speaker tell a joke I've heard before. All I can focus on is how it's being told and how it compares to how I originally heard it. The only way to be certain humor is fresh is to talk creatively from your own life. This way, there's no way they could have heard it before. But we'll look at humor more later.

8. Delve into a technical story.

"And there I was, using an SQL debugger and it turns out that the database was pure IDMS!"

A great story...if your audience happens to be entirely comprised of I.T. staff who have been in the industry since the early 1990's. For anyone else, though, even if they *are* sharp enough to figure out roughly what the problem was, they still won't *relate* to it. And there's just a hint of a sense of elitism when you act like you expect them to be knowledgeable about the topic.

At my grandfather's funeral, I told a story of a very touching moment relating to him and was surprised to get almost no reaction. Afterward, my cousin said to me, "That was a really cool story and I bet everyone in the room would have thought so too...if they had any idea what a Palm Pilot was." I looked around the room at a group of people predominantly over 80 and realized that she was right; if one didn't know what a Palm Pilot was, the story made no sense.

9. Comment on the people who are not paying attention.

"Excuse me! The man in the fourth row! Is this all making sense to you? I noticed you looking around." Yikes! Let it go. Maybe he's got more on his mind than you know. From my experience, it's not worth interrupting your flow to vie for someone's attention.

If there is a group that have not stopped chatting and you know it will be a distraction, you can look in that direction and smile until they pick up on the fact that you were waiting for quiet. They'll get the idea quickly and you'll look professional for having waited so long as there isn't a *hint* of scolding in your face.

There is *one* tactic for gaining an individuals attention that works great with kids and can be used tactfully with adults. It can only be used, though, if you know the people in your audience, including the person who seems distracted, or if you can read a name tag on the person:

There are some clever tricks to regain audience members' attention without having to embarrass them...or yourself!

Referring to the person by name *without* actually calling upon him tends to snap the person back to focus without seeming catty. If Wendell looks half-asleep or appears distracted as I'm speaking about customer service, for instance, I could change my example on the fly to:

"Let's say that Kathleen is a customer and, when she calls, Wendell answers the phone. In the first ten seconds, Wendell needs to..."

Without pointing out in any way that he looked distracted, I'm betting you'll have his complete focus now.

10.   Do anything that expects a high energy participatory response.

"Hey everybody! I'm Milo! First, pull out a pen and write down ten things you know about customer service. Then turn to the person next to you and share your lists. Then we'll all stand up and stretch. Then..."

Oof! I love interactive programs, but take some time to talk and develop a little rapport before getting them to participate.

So by not committing these ten mistakes, we have an excellent chance of getting through the opening. The only little thing we have left is the next 98% of our program. But hey, it's no small thing to do well in the first 2%!

Now let's look at ways we can do well by our audience. Or, just to make reading this a little more fun, let's look at ten ways we could potentially *alienate* them...and then please do the opposite!

10

10 Neat Things To Talk About If You WANT To Alienate Your Audience

While you can't please everyone, there are things you can do that will certainly stack the odds against you. I've seen BIG names say things that were so unnecessary and alienate much of the room in the process. I had one woman lean over toward me after a comment made by a celebrity speaker and whisper, "If that's how he feels, I don't care how great his materials are supposed to be, I'm not giving him one dollar of MY money!"

So, should you WANT to alienate your audience, here's ten things you can talk about to accomplish that (or, if you're sane, it's ten things you should avoid).

1. Sex.

It's amazing to me just how sensitive people can be on this topic, but it's not my place to judge. If you even *question* a statement's chance of offending someone, there's a possibility that there will be people in the room who are not offended but will bristle because they worry that *others* will react.

These might be the people who have the power to hire you again. Don't give them reason to *worry* that someone *else* in room might be uncomfortable, even if they are wrong.

It can take so little! I told a story once that made *reference* to a bra. Not on a woman; just as an article of clothing I encountered in a box. I noticed a table of mature women lose their smiles at that moment. Apparently, bras are not mentioned in their world of polite company.

---

2.   **Drugs, in any positive light.**

It doesn't matter if the story is forty years old or if you were in Amsterdam where it's legal, we are not living in a time where drugs can be mentioned from the platform in any kind of positive light.

The exception, alcohol, must be referenced cautiously. Keep in mind that, in almost every audience, there are both active and reformed drinkers, family members of alcoholics, people with deep regrets about something they did under the influence, and family members of victims of drunk drivers.

I'm not saying you can't bring up alcohol, but think it through before deciding if you need that story...or at least the fact that alcohol was involved.

---

3.   **Politics, unless you can do it neutrally.**

In the story I mentioned at the beginning of this chapter, it was a speaker so full of himself that he thought he could disrespect one of the two main political parties because the audience surely was filled with *his* kind of people. What he did instead was convince half of the room that they were *not* his kind of people.

In my book, "The Worst Days Make The Best Stories", there's an anecdote about what happened when a client accidentally found out that I was endorsing a specific candidate. As it was easier to tell the story using a name than avoiding being specific, I named the presidential candidate "Berry" — blending Bush and Kerry into one name so as not to alienate the readers. It mattered not to the story which candidate I endorsed — just that he disagreed and supported "Kush".

---

4.   **Tell only "How Great Am I?" stories.**

Although excessive humility can be exhausting to listen to, it's usually better to err on that side than to appear to be bragging.

That being said, it doesn't mean you can't tell stories where things went well for you. Just keep a balance. I do tell one story where I saw the right solution when no one else did. The bragging factor is somewhat tempered by the fact that the story clearly takes place over twenty years ago and that the point of the story is the way I *shared* the idea, not that I was the one that *had* the idea. I also usually close with a self-deprecating story where I don't end up coming off so well, which gives a little balance.

---

5.   **Bad mouth competitors, especially by name!**

This just looks petty, especially when they aren't there to defend themselves.

Of course, if you're doing a sales presentation, the rules are a little different, but focus comparisons on product and service, not people or reputations.

---

6.   **Tell inside jokes that are funny to only a few people in attendance.**

"...and there I was, stuck downtown, thinking, 'If only Alicia Maltese were here!'" (Chuckles from one corner) "Those of you who have been on the steering committee know what I'm talking about."

Great. But the rest of the room feels left out. If the inside joke is that good, share it with those who would get it *afterward*.

In "The Worst Days Make The Best Stories", I share a tale of a substitute rabbi in my temple who told a ten minute long joke and then the punch line was in Yiddish! Almost no one got the joke and we were all distracted afterward, trying to find out what the line meant instead of concentrating on the prayers that followed.

7. Mention how little something costs or how much money people should have.

"...and I can't imagine why anyone wouldn't have high speed internet when it only costs about $45 a month!"

For the many people in the room who are only making the minimum payment on their credit cards, $45 a month could be a lot - this kind of statement can seem demeaning.

That same big speaker I mentioned earlier said, at another point in his program, "and you owe it to yourself not to do *anything* that pays you less than $50 an hour!"

That's $100,000 a year. I'm betting there were a *lot* of people in the room making less with no recourse to get anywhere close to such a figure. He just looked pompous telling them they were missing the boat to success.

8. Anything that makes you look too full of yourself.

"...So there I was, in the south of France, snacking on truffles and brie with Robert DeNiro, Princess Anne, and Omar Sharif, when I realized that I was wearing *last year's tuxedo*! Hyuk Hyuk..."

Impress the audience with your platform skills, not life details you can brag about. They'll get more out of your program if they can *relate* to you than be impressed by what you have, what you've done, and who you met along the way.

Besides, those of us who are *really* friends with Princess Anne *know* she doesn't like brie. ☺

9. Point out anything that's wrong with the event or audience.

I'll let comments like these speak for themselves. Would you want to hear any of these if you were in the audience?

- "I'm happy to be with you today, though I think this is the last time I'll come to Cleveland in January. I'm not sure how you put up with this kind of cold!"

- "I wanted to spend some time on five ways we could we could boost sales this quarter, but the announcements this morning went way over their schedule, so I just don't have time now."

- "I'll list five management concerns and hope those of you in the back can hear over this crummy speaker system."

- "The problem with your company, "BigCo" is that you don't..."

Hey, how about that buffet? Reminds me of the slop from high school!

Don't complain about things that have gone wrong.

Sometimes a comment is simply unnecessary, like the one knocking Cleveland. Other times, a problem needs to be acknowledged, but can be done in a positive way. Here are some more positive ways the other three could be stated:

- "In the time that I have, I can only hit some of the highlights of this topic, but I can share more details afterward."

- "I'll be listing five management concerns and, as a few of you in the back mentioned that it's a little hard to hear, I'll go slower than I normally would. If you miss anything, feel free to email me and I'll either write back or, if I hear from a number of you, I'll post information on my website.."

- "One of the things that LittleCo is getting positive media attention for is _____. I understand that BigCo hasn't implemented a similar plan yet, but it may be worth looking at seeing if it could be a cash cow for you as well."

---

10.   Bring up anything you're bitter about.

"Financial planning is a key part of your security blanket. Of course, if you have an ex-wife like mine, you can forget most of that security and plan to work well into your seventies. Apparently, the laws of this state don't seem to care who…"

I think you get the picture. Inappropriate.

Wow…that flew by…with so much more to say! There's so many little things I've seen go wrong on this front. Let's do ten more!

11

10 *More* Things You Can Do To Alienate Your Audience

Those first ten points all made sense, right? Hopefully, this chapter should be just as sensible.

1.   Stay behind the lectern or a table.

What's the difference between being outside on a nice day and looking at the same nice day through a large window? It's a disconnect - you don't feel as related to it.

It's the same with the lectern. It's a physical barrier between you and your audience. Some people say they feel vulnerable without the lectern — good! There's a reason for that; you *are* more vulnerable and the audience knows it. And because of that, the audience is more open, respectful, connected, and responsive. That's what we really want.

Besides the security of being mostly hidden behind the lectern, there's another reason we tend to like using it. notes. It's true that you have to work a little harder to be able to leave that safety zone. I'm not saying you can never step behind it, but do so to check notes, if you must, and then step back out. Ideally, with good preparation and PowerPoint, you shouldn't be in a position of having to read much at all.

By the way, there's no law that says the audience has to see your slides. If you cannot do a PowerPoint show for some reason, you can still have a laptop and remote to walk yourself through your program. The notes are bright and clear for you while you remain front and center.

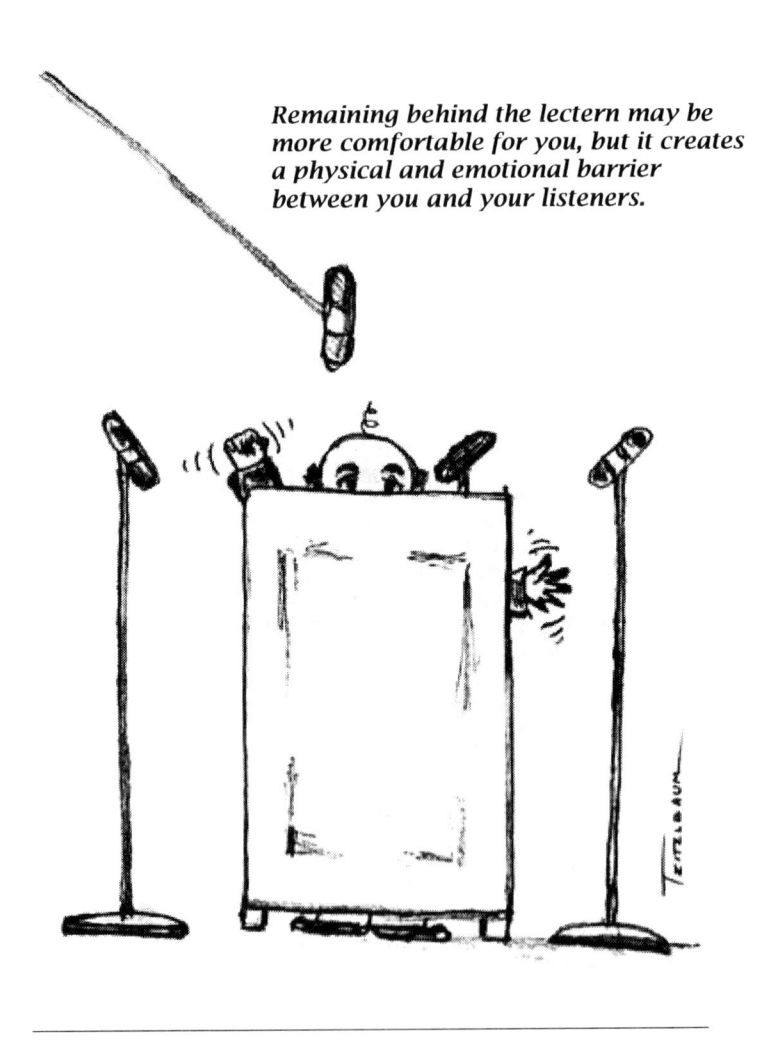

Remaining behind the lectern may be more comfortable for you, but it creates a physical and emotional barrier between you and your listeners.

2. **Talk to the back wall.**

At one point, speakers were frequently given this terrible advice: Avoid favoring the front rows by looking beyond the last row while you are speaking.

This does not endear you to the back of the audience. It simply makes you look disconnected from *everyone*.

Make eye contact with those that you can in as wide a range as you can see. If there are sections beyond your sight, speak at times to the mass of heads in that area, just to acknowledge that you appreciate their being there — even if you can't make eye contact.

One of the surprisingly true lessons I learned early in my career is that the audience actually feels far more connected to you if you are looking at one person in the house than if you look at nobody. Somehow, energetically, when you connect with one person, there's a feeling that you are connected to the group through that person, especially if you maintain that eye contact just a bit longer than you would typically before going on to the next person.

---

3. **Make extremely long eye contact with someone in the audience.**

When I say in the last point that we can connect better sometimes by holding eye contact "just a bit longer", I'm talking about going from three seconds all the way up to about five.

If you stick to one person much longer than that, you may unnerve them and that energy can carry to the room as people feel uncomfortable for that person.

---

4. **Make all your eye contact, however long, with just one person.**

It's important to vary where you look. Choosing one person for too long can appear to be favoritism, inappropriate attraction, a misleading impression that this person need to hear the message more than others...share the connection!

---

5. Fail to personalize *any* of your stories.

No matter what your topic, taking a moment to humanize yourself as it relates to the topic can make you more appreciated as a speaker.

So what do you do if you're speaking on a topic that is very fact-based and isn't about you personally? *Find* your own connection to it:

"...and so it seems possible after all that the hubenfluben virus could very well be the cause of Mergatroid Syndrome. Now I realize that seems surprising, given the many years we've treated it as a common cell disorder. Indeed, I actually spoke to several of my peers and asked them if I'd be putting my reputation on the line to even share this theory, but there does seem to be enough evidence of the viral theory that I felt I had to take that chance — if only to let you know that it merits discussion."

The facts haven't been lost, but a personal connection to them has been created, bringing the speaker into the issue.

---

6. Make frequent reference to running out of time

"Wow, look at the time...oh, how much time do I have left now?... boy, the time's sure going fast...okay let me see if I can rush through this last part..."

Eventually, the audience is going to feel like they are being rushed and/or cheated out of what you would have given them if you hadn't been pressed for time.

---

7. Make random movements that don't match what you're talking about.

In our attempt not to look stiff, we learn to try to move our bodies more. But in the pendulum of learning, we can go too far the other way, especially if our movements don't match what we're saying.

Imagine the speaker with arms wide open saying, "...and she had the tiniest little puppy with her." Her mouth is saying "tiny" while her arms are saying "huge".

And it's a shame that she *could* have achieved an appropriate and interesting image by drawing her head into her shoulders and scrunching her elbows in toward her ribs, making herself look tiny, like the puppy would have.

---

8. Make low status choices that emphasize your discomfort.

We haven't addressed the issue of status directly yet. It is a term used in improvisation to refer to the level of control that characters seem to have over one another.

For instance, in "The Wizard of Oz", the actor playing the Cowardly Lion emphasized his character's low status feelings by shifting weight, turning inward, talking into his shoulder, rambling, pouting, and more. Dorothy, by contrast, showed she was a strong little girl by standing firmly planted, raising her chest, and speaking succinctly in a clear voice.

Taken to the speaker's platform, we want to appear in a place of high status most of the time (unless we're telling a story where we're portraying ourselves or another in a low status situation).

Low status actions to avoid include:

- aimless wandering
- touching your face unnecessarily
- playing with your hair
- turning feet inward
- slumping shoulders forward
- sighing
- apologizing where it isn't called for
- over-the-top humility
- saying "uh" or "um" before sentences
- blushing

The last one may seem out of one's control, but doing what you can to avoid setting yourself up for embarrassment can certainly help.

---

9. Face the screen to read your PowerPoint slides.

This error manifests itself in two ways. Either you have your back to the audience too much or you are spinning back and forth like a lawn sprinkler.

Whenever possible, have the computer where you can see it so you needn't see the screen at all. If that's not possible in larger settings, ask for a "confidence monitor" — an extra monitor that can be hooked up to show exactly what's on the screen.

---

10. Make generalizations about groups in society.

I certainly would hope that most of us know better than to tell jokes that would have been told thirty years ago. Jokes about particular ethnicities, religious groups, and other stereotyping humor have no place on the stage.

This may seem too obvious to bring up, but with each decade that passes, we become a little more aware. I've seen people who would never tell a joke about the handicapped or an ethnic group get on stage and offend people with offhanded comments regarding age, gender, sexual orientation, or weight. These topics haven't become taboo for humor yet, but that doesn't mean people aren't taking offense.

My friend Michael and his wife were at a party. One of the guests, "George", told a joke wherein one of the characters was gay and the punch line reflected this in a negative manner, which was supposed to be why it was funny. Several people laughed but Michael spoke up, saying, "Excuse me, but as someone who has a gay brother, I don't know why you'd assume I'd find that funny."

George tried to back-paddle with the standard, "Hey, lighten up...it was just a joke..." but he could now see that he hadn't come off well. Even if we think we know who is present, we don't know the people who are close to them, be it their overweight child, their aging parent, their sister struggling with a glass ceiling, or their gay friend.

Over the course of the party, two individuals and another married couple came over and told Michael that they were glad he said something because the joke had made them uncomfortable as well, but they hadn't felt comfortable to speak up. In fact, one of those who came over was someone who *had* laughed, primarily out of feeling awkward.

And had Michael not commented, the laughs and polite smiles they *would* have given George would have empowered him to continue this behavior, never recognizing that he was alienating people further.

Okay, now you're prepared to avoid a lot of potential pitfalls. You're organizing your speech, but knowing that more people are *visual* learners than *auditory* or kinesthetic (intuitive) learners, you do plan to have visual components. I hope?

Luckily, since you're reading a book, I'll never know if the answer was "uh...no..." and there's still time for you to plan some visual aspects to your presentation.

So now that we'll change that "No" to "Of course!", let's look at some of the ways to use them effectively...(or not!)

12
10 Great Ways to Blow It With Visuals

Now, even having *just* said how important visual tools are for your more visual-learning attendees, I'd rather see you do your entire program without them than have you use them poorly!

It's not hard to use them well, especially once we review some of the mistakes I've seen people make (yes...yes...including me...)

1. **Forget that you are a speaker and think your visuals *are* your presentation.**

Throw a chart up there and talk around it. After all, why discuss it at all if you've shown it to them?

I saw someone do that with a blueprint one time. Having assumed that we all learned what we needed to without discussion, he went on to the next slide. I had only a vague idea what he thought I was supposed to have gotten from that picture.

2. **Use fonts and objects that only some of the audience can see.**

If you can see it, surely it's good enough for everyone, right? Wrong. Account for the fact that some of your attendees, may not be able to see as clearly as you can — even if you check it from the back of the room.

Creative fonts should only be used for short headings. Not only can they be hard to read, but even for those who can, it slows the brain down to process the different look. You've distracted them away from quickly getting the information and coming back to listening to YOU!

> Do *you* see what I *mean?*
> This MAY SEeM like A
> GROss exaGgeration, but I
> think you get the point.

3. **Fill your displays with nothing but text.**

Dreary, dreary, dreary! It takes very little effort to put some related picture on a slide and you'd be amazed how just a little visual can hold people's attention more, especially if you can use a little humor to intrigue them.

4. Put lots of points on one slide or overhead.

Our brains go into overload when we see too much at once. Whether it's a PowerPoint slide, overheads, charts, or props, keep visuals simple and then go deeper over time if necessary.

When showing slides, I realize that there's a desire to group similar concepts on one screen to show the common ground, but that doesn't mean that all seven points have to be detailed on the same slide. More on that in our PowerPoint chapter.

---

5. Put everything you'll say on the slide and read it to us.

Titles and bullets. That's all you need and all they want to see. It's dreary to have someone read detailed slides to us. The details have to come out in your speaking.

---

6. Do everything in black-and-white.

After all, why stimulate their senses with that newfangled invention called "color" when you can just as easily bore them with lots of fully accurate black-and-white slides?

Start spoiling them with color and the next thing you know, they'll start expecting you to stop talking in monotone too!

---

7. Hold things that have no relationship to what you're saying.

If the audience doesn't get why you're holding something, that's what they'll be thinking about instead of what you're saying.

While props can be a nice addition, it's only true if they fit the moment! Avoid picking them up until you're about to or have already referenced them.

---

8. Hold things that you chose for your presentation long after you've stopped referring to them.

This isn't as bad as the last one, but if you're using your arms and hands effectively, they are going to be moving. So flailing the soccer trophy that was appropriate in your opening story ten minutes ago is not a good choice. When you're done with a prop, return it to the lectern or some other safe place.

---

9. Wave things around so everyone can see them, if only for a fraction of a second at a time

Whoosh! Was that a prop? I have no idea. If you're going to bother to bring something, show it gentle and long enough for people to take it in.

---

10. Use so many props that you will fumble with them as you go between them.

You've only got two hands so proper usage of your props is enough of a challenge — especially if one hand might be dedicated to a microphone. Choose the most effective props and make sure you'll have ample time to put one down before needing that hand for another.

This includes mimed props! When I first started speaking, I never counted on a remote for PowerPoint (now I bring my own in case theirs doesn't work). Since I would press enter to advance slides, my hands were free. The first time I was given a remote, I loved the fact that I could get away from the computer but it hadn't occurred to me that one of my hands was now bound to the remote!

As I began gesturing and miming the action of my story, I reached a point where I realized I needed both hands free but I was stuck with the remote. I had to run back to the lectern to drop it off and then come back to my story in order to finish it. Now I make a point of walking toward the lectern earlier in that story to drop off the remote so my hands will be free when I need them.

Now that we're done talking about what you'll be holding, let's spend some time talking about what the audience may be holding: your handouts!

13

10 Hot Tips for Handouts

Handouts fall into that "can't live with 'em; can't without 'em" category for many speakers. The down side is that they are a distraction, a pain to distribute, a bother to make, and can't be changed on the fly. The positives, which can't be overlooked, are that they help people keep focus on what you think is important, leave attendees with better notes, and give them your contact info.

Only you can decide if the good outweighs the bad, but here are ten points that can help you succeed on this issue.

1. **Make a conscious decision when to pass them out.**

Pros and cons again here, but at least know that up front so you can make the best choice. There are three basic options:

Option 1: In Advance

I don't mean on a different day — that's just begging for people to forget them! I mean so that they get a packet upon arriving which includes your materials and any others for the event surrounding yours, if there are other speakers or business.

This tends to be my favorite because there's no distraction issue and they have them at their seats when you start.

The considerations are:

a. You have to get them to someone in advance. This person has to be willing to and adept at getting them handed out. Not long ago, I sent the handouts in advance to a meeting planner. When I arrived at 10 am, ready to go on at 11 (which was three hours into their meeting), she handed me the pile of handouts and said, "How are you going to give these out?" I thought she'd done it before I arrived!

b. There's no changing them once the client has run off copies.

c. I've had to stop mid-story to point out that I do have handouts that they should be following because they didn't know I had stuff in their packet.

Option 2: Just before you go on

If you're the first or only person on the program, this is about the same situation as option 1. If not, and you show up later in the program, you do have the option to hand out your materials between speakers.

Handouts can either be a great resource that complement your program or just another form of distraction.

It's all in how you use them.

The advantage of this is that they are fresh into their hands and they are ready to use them with you.

The disadvantage, to me, is bigger. It's that it's a panic to get them out quickly and it's either dead time while you do this or you are distracting from the previous speaker's time.

I try to do this only with very small groups. If you've got twelve people to address, for instance, it's no biggie to have them passed out in between programs and then it's fresh in their hands as a reminder to look at it while you're sharing.

Option 3: During your program, as needed

The last option is to give each section out as it is about to be references.

The disadvantages are clear: it's a huge distraction, cuts into the flow of your program, leads to side chatter, and takes time from your program. But there are times when this process can be worthwhile:

 a. There are some programs where attendees who look ahead may undermine something you want to do up front. Scheduled handouts prevent this.

 b. If you're sure that something further into your handout will be a distraction that will have people reading instead of listening, it's a reason to use this method.

 c. There may be situations where you have a little bit of time to fill or know that you need a moment set up something. The passing out of more handouts can give you these time fillers.

If you are going to use this method, here are a few recommendations for success:

- Unless the group is tiny, don't do it yourself. Have a designated person(s) who will, on your cue, head down the aisle(s) and give out the next batch to pass down.
- A faster method is to have the piles at the end of the rows in a color coded format. Then all you have to say is, "We're moving on to the yellow handout. Would the people on the aisle please take one and pass them down?"

- If you're willing to trust them, you can do the color coding at their seats: "That wraps up the white handout. Please pull the blue one out of your folder now." Be forewarned, though: some are still going to read the pink one while you're talking.

2.   **Spellcheck them.**

And then proofread them...because spellchecking is only so useful when typos can lead to other real words. If eye reed won moor sentence width typos that r reel words butt knot the word the author untended two use...get the point?

This is especially true if you use voice recognition software. Recently, I dictated a letter into my email program. Instead of the bland salutation "Sincerely, Milo", I opted to say something a bit more original, ending with "Warmly, Milo". Thank goodness I proofread it; the software had interpreted my voice into the words "Orally, Milo"! I might have gotten away with that salutation as a professional speaker, but it still sounds pretty odd!

3.   **Keep references short.**

The handouts you go over are for quick reference and introducing concepts. Keep them short, crisp, and thin.

"But wait," you say! I have information I want them to read later and in more detail than I can go over from the platform!" Wonderful. Almost by definition, these lend themselves to two places, ***appendices*** and ***website links***:

- **Appendix A-Z**

    I'm not saying you can't give them more info than you can cover. I'm saying don't put that material in the *body* of what you ARE covering.

    If you're talking about flammable pajamas for a couple of minutes, stick to what they need to know and add: "See Appendix A for a list of credible manufacturers and Appendix B for an article in the New York Times about safe ways to test for flammability." Boom. Done. They have the info but the handout stays on track.

- **Website links**

    Does anyone need just a little more paper in their homes or offices? If you can supply a link to the info for them to read more later, that's all they need in many cases.

    And if you're in business for yourself, it's an excuse to drive traffic to your website if you post the info on your OWN site. The page in question has to clearly hold the info you've promised, but there's nothing wrong with a link at the bottom saying, "This article written by Nancy Smith. To learn more about Nancy and her speeches about the tree bark diet plan, click here."

    The only risk of links instead of paper is that they may never read it. So it's up to you to decide how much you care about that. If you seriously care that they read it (i.e.: it furthers some cause for you), make it an appendix as they are more likely to read it. If you just want to be thorough but it's no skin off your nose if they accept your higher level speech, save a tree and just give them a link.

---

4. **Include appropriate, pleasing visuals**

Remember that you've got those visual learners out there. Better to split material over two screens and put a visual with each than leave the visual off to "make room".

There are so many sites with clip art (including great options in Word and PowerPoint) that there's just no reason not to use them. The catch can be finding just the right picture to go with your point or story.

Some products, like Word, allow you to search on a word. If the story involves an important phone call, search on "phone" and you'll likely find numerous pictures of people on a call, one of which may work well.

And it need not be an item or an action! You can search for "angry", "chaos", "helpful", and other such themes to see what pictures have been put with such terms.

---

5.   **Leave room.**

No matter how thorough you are, attendees like to take notes between lines and in margins.

---

6.   **Put your direct contact info in the footnote of every page.**

Pages come apart. Covers come off. My footnote has my email, website, and company name on *every* page.

I used to include the phone number, too, but I find that sending people to the website answers their questions better and faster than I can orally. And the phone number is on the site, if they still need to call me.

---

7.   **Put page numbers in the footnote.**

They are helpful for you to reference during the speech and so attendees can refer to them during Q&A.

---

8.   **Have an extra handout for yourself that is an exact copy of theirs.**

I often have an old "teacher's edition" of the handouts with my notes all over it. But if I've customized the handout for them, it's nice to be able to look at their version to have their matching page number since mine might be different.

---

9. Use color.

It's a simple thing to do, if color copies are a reasonable choice. If not, consider at least a color cover or even printing the cover on a colored sheet.

---

10. Use a fill-in the blank format to keep people engaged.

Try handouts that have fill-ins, like: "Put page numbers in the _____". When people have to write a bit, they are more likely to be engaged. They don't want to miss any of the fill-in moments.

It can be abused, though — one speaker I saw had us writing so much that it was hard to keep up with him. I recommend one key word per heading and/or main point. But if you're going to be moving quickly through a section, complete your sentences in that area orally, so people don't feel like they missed something.

And since people will still daydream or get distracted, I always have the non-blank fill in on my website for those who'd like to find out what they missed.

So now you're ready for a pleasing, helpful, organized handout. But back to the speech: what about organizing that? Okay, that's our next topic.

14

10 Sensible Ways to Organize Your Program

This is not a comprehensive list, but it may give you some ideas you haven't had before.

Most presentations will fall into one of these categories whether you intended for them to or not, so it's not a bad idea to be conscious of which one you've selected so you can make sure you are consistent.

1. Chronologically.

Take the events you need to discuss from a beginning point in time to the end point.

2. Biggest to smallest.

Describe the grandest physical scale of the topic and then fine tune as the program goes on. For a hotel, for instance, talking about the numbers of guests, major events, and hotel features up front could work and then drilling down to finer focus, like customer service specifics, dining room specialties, etc.

Smallest to biggest can work as well.

3.   **Most significant to least.**

What's biggest in size might not be what's biggest in significance. A program can be organized from the most important issues down to smaller ones...or the reverse for a big ending.

---

4.   **Most (adjective) to least.**

Items two and three are the most obvious examples of this, but one can put almost any describing word there and go up or down in scale: most successful, most rewarding, most fun, most well-known, etc., depending on the topic at hand.

---

5.   **Universally to locally.**

This is a nice one because people see the pattern but it's not as commonly done. Talking about what we're doing, then what our region is doing, and then what the whole company is doing, for instance, ties the relevance together. As does starting companywide and fine tuning it down to the actions of those present.

---

6.   **Background / Problem / Proposal.**

This is similar to chronological because it is a past, present, future format, but it is fine-tuned to be centered on a specific issue.

Keeping this in mind can make sure that the earlier sections are used only to support the problem (or situation) and the proposal that you are putting before the group.

---

7.   **Story / Call to action.**

Let your audience get caught up in the emotion of a story you tell that leads them to the interpretation you would hope for. Then talk about what they/we can do to make this happen.

This works well in very short presentations or as a *section* of a larger speech; if you have to speak for an hour, I don't recommend a 45 minute story with a fifteen minute call to action!

---

8. Acronym.

Acronyms are a nice way to make points memorable. Think of the key word that describes each section of your presentation and see if you can arrange them into a word. If not, perhaps you can find a synonym for one of them.

It's nice if you can make it a word that is on topic. If you're doing a sales presentation, maybe they spell out V-A-L-U-E) because that makes it easier to remember and associate. Take the same presentation and have the points spell out W-O-R-M-S...well, there's a bit of a disconnect there (unless you're in the bait business).

If you can't make a great fitting word, YOU be the connection. Use a graphic that shows worms coming out of a can and talk about the fact that every great sales program has some worms in it somewhere. That's your transition to the W-O-R-M-S acronym and it's made your program a little lighter.

Try not to exceed five letters if you're going to discuss each point. I heard a speaker use the acronym C-E-L-E-B-R-A-T-I-O-N and I saw the look on people's faces: "Holy cow, this is going to take forever to get through!" Luckily, she had only about a sentence on each letter so it went quickly, but by the time she got to those last few letters, it was clear that she was forcing the synonyms a bit just to finish her acronym!

---

9. Number/letter combination.

As an alternative to the acronym, you can use a number/letter combination. This looks like "The 4 B's of Customer Service" or "The 5 P's of Jam Making".

In my case, for instance, I created the "5 C's of Teamwork and Rapport™":

The 5 C's of Teamwork and Rapport™:
Creativity
Cooperation
Communication
Commitment
Community

Having announced it, I can work through each one in discussion. Acronyms are actually easier for you and the audience to remember (I've occasionally gotten four of my five C's and blanked on the fifth...thank goodness for PowerPoint!). It's easier to remember each of the five words that go with W-O-R-M-S than it is to remember all five C's.

So why'd I go with this method if it's not quite as effective? Because all the things I was thinking of were C words. It was easier to accept that than to force all five points into other words that don't start with C.

Another nice thing about acronyms and number/letter formats is that it sets expectations on time. The audience has a sense of how much longer this example will go on if you're up to the letter "M" in W-O-R-M-S.

10. Any other way that feels right and powerful.

This is my catch-all point, allowing me to say that there are many other ideas on organization and if you have a good one for your topic, by all means use it! As long as you're conscious of *what* your organization method is so you are consistent in using it.

In point number 9, I brought up the dreaded P word: PowerPoint!

In case you're not familiar with the term, it's good to know that there are competing softwares that do the same thing, but like Kleenex and Jell-o, the brand name has become synonymous with the concept. A PowerPoint presentation is a computer generated series of slides that go along with a presentation. It's the modern day equivalent of using an overhead projector...and way better!

PowerPoint is loved and it's hated, but it's here to stay. So instead of fearing it...let's maximize its potential!

15

10 Smart Ways to Maximize Your PowerPoint Experience

Not since the great "stand-behind-the-lectern-or-not" debate of the 1980s has a topic so divided the speaking community: To PowerPoint or not to PowerPoint...that is the question still being debated within the National Speakers Association.

Unfortunately, it is one of the questions with no true answer. Should a speaker be *so* dynamic and clear that there's simply no reason to use PowerPoint? Or should we be realistic about the different learning styles which include visual learners and use a tool like PowerPoint to be sure to reach everyone?

I lean heavily toward the latter, though I've certainly seen powerful speakers who never lost their audience for a minute without the tool. So why do I favor it? Because I've seen so many speakers benefit from effective use of it AND there's relatively non-users that I think would have been hurt *by* using it. Perhaps it would have made them even better.

There are only two real downsides to using PowerPoint: the time to develop a good program and the possibility of technology headaches. With good precautions, neither should be a reason to avoid PowerPoint, so let's look at how to use it best!

1.   Set the right click button for reverse.

Whether it's for the program itself or for your own practice, at some point you will be using the left mouse click to advance slides. Did you know that the right mouse can be set to be a reverse button so that you can go back one slide?

To set it:

a. Go to the Tools menu on the main menu bar.
b. Select Options.
c. Under the View tab, go to the Slide show section.
d. Uncheck the box labeled:
   "Popup menu on right mouse click."

It's easy to set and you only have to do it once for a given computer. Frankly, I can't imagine why it's not the default because, once I show the option to people, I'm yet to have someone not want it that way.

---

2. **Get a remote!**

Sure we can make the mouse a little better, but why be held by your computer to press the Enter key constantly? A remote frees you to move about and be more natural in your speaking style.

Cost is no longer a reason not to have one. I bought one on eBay last year for under $20 with shipping! It comes with me to every event. Sure enough, there have been at least three times when the client's remote hasn't worked and my USB remote was connected in a few minutes, saving the day.

One end plugs into a USB port as a receiver and the other sits in your hand. They keep getting smaller, too. Mine is about the size of a digital thermometer and takes care of forward, backward, and laser pointing. Better models also allow you to make the screen go black in case you want to walk where the screen would be showing (it's unflattering to walk around with words across your face and body).

One caution: if the receiver is blocked by the laptop screen, it may not pick up the signal. For under $10, I use a USB extension cord that allows me to put the receiver along the side of the laptop where it isn't blocked. It also gives me two additional USB ports.

---

3.   **Take your own photos.**

Using only the illustrations that come with PowerPoint can be limiting and begin to look stale. Take digital photos of family, friends, and places that matter to you so that your program feels fresh and personal.

When I'm talking about my family, my audiences get a kick out of a 1981 picture of my father and me...including my mass of dark brown hair shaped like a giant helmet.

Use real pictures that you have taken or gotten permission to use, instead of just the ones that come as clip art.

4.   **Add humor with a great visual to lead into a story.**

I tell one story about a client who instituted a program called the "Screw Up Of The Month" club. Initially, the slide just had that title and got little response. After hearing a program about using more visuals in PowerPoint, I looked at that slide and wondered what I could do with it.

I ended up putting two cartoons together: one of a giant screw and another of a surprised-looking face just above it, as if he had committed a big screw-up. It almost always gets a laugh now and all that I invested was a little creativity.

---

5. **Simple or no transitions.**

The days of impressing people with sliding, spinning, or bouncing slide transitions is way behind us. It's nothing more than a distraction.

When you're done with a slide, just have the next one come up. The option to do this is called "None".

If you do pick a transition for some reason, be consistent. Use the same one throughout.

---

6. **Simple animations *that stop* are great.**

Little juggling men, bouncing kitties, and fireworks all look neat-o, but after the first couple of seconds they become nothing but a distraction. A bit of movement is okay, so long as it's something that stops quickly so attention stays on you.

I saw someone speak recently who had so much motion in his presentation that it was hard to pay attention to him and what was on the screen. If there's something happening on the screen that you *want* them to focus on, like a video, your comments need to be minimal during it.

By comparison, a chart that grows is nice. Show the first quarter profits. Press the button and add the second quarter profits to it on the same screen. That's just good graphic usage, not added confusion.

---

7. Match fill-ins with a consistent pattern that shows the missing words.

If your handout has a spot that says:

> Greet customers with a _____.

there should be a corresponding PowerPoint slide that says:

> Greet customers with a **smile.**

Notice that I left the underline so that it was clear to those in listening mode that it was time to go back to the handout for a fill-in. Likewise, for the more visual learners, the visual clue will tune them in better to the listening when they realize an answer is being given.

---

8. Don't show all your upcoming text at once.

If you have a lot to say on a topic that could appear on one slide, you have two good alternatives to an overwhelming slide of, say, seven points:

<u>Appear-on-click</u>: First just show the title, say "Seven Great Ways To Deal With Classroom Discipline" as you introduce the topic. Then, have PowerPoint display each point as you are ready to discuss it. After your introduction, you click your remote or mouse and point #1 either appears or flies from the right into position for you to talk about. Continue through all seven points that way.

<u>Multiple screens</u>: Put your title and the seven points on eight different screens. Be sure you number each point even though it's on its own screen so that it's clear that you are still working on that topic list. With this method, I recommend a nice summary slide after the last point that lists the seven aforementioned points with no details. Even if it's only up there for a few seconds, it just has a nice finishing feel to your list.

By the way, if you use the multiple screens method, there's not going to be much on each screen, is there? What a great place to find a fun or interesting picture that reflects the point on that screen!

---

9. Read any significant words aloud.

Don't assume that because you've put the words on screen that they are reading, especially if they have handouts or other distractions.

---

10. Use PowerPoint to cheat!

PowerPoint is your biggest memorization friend. There's very little that you can't put onto PowerPoint to avoid having to memorize it if you construct your display carefully.

That isn't to say that you should put every word up there or that you shouldn't work to know as much as you can! But there are times when you KNOW it ain't gonna happen without some notes. So instead of fumbling with paper or index cards, use PowerPoint to your advantage!

For instance, I once applied to give a speech at an international conference and was accepted. I had a 60 minute program ready to go, but their acceptance letter informed me that my timeslot was 90 minutes! With some creativity, I found a way to tie in some more advanced material and fill the time nicely, but it was a lot to have ready to deliver in a short time.

I was working with a ten point list like the ones in this book, so it was easy to put one on each screen and include a good graphic. I knew what I wanted to say about each point but I was having trouble remembering how I wanted to start each section.

Finally, I got smart and put a sentence on the bottom of the screen that reminded me of how I wanted to start out. I actually put a line like "Suppose you called your local phone company..." and *said those words*. Then I went on with what I wanted to say. It eliminated the risk of my forgetting how to start out.

I asked someone later if it was distracting. She said she assumed it was there as a lead-in for *them*. Solved my problem and harmed nothing. A nice little cheat!

So PowerPoint can be a friend for you and for your audience. But as I said, it's no replacement for rehearsal to be ready to do good work.

Ugh! Rehearsal??? That sounds like work. Afraid so. But with some good tips on rehearsal skills it might not be so bad after all.

16

10 Gold Nuggets for Rehearsing

For all of my years of improvisation work and knowing how much fun and how exciting it can be to create "on the fly", I must break the bad news:

While the ability to improvise *can* get you out of trouble and *can* help you create new ideas, it's no substitute for planning and rehearsal when it comes to speaking. In fact, it helps you better improvise if the moment is right because you know just how to veer off the path and get back on again...because the path is clear.

Realistically, it's not so easy to run though an entire speech as practice...and then do it again...and then do it again... Especially if it's an hour long program!

Let's go over a number of ideas that can make that time more efficient, successful, and enjoyable.

1.   **Get away from the mirror!**

Somewhere along the way, someone probably told you that a great way to learn about your speaking skills is to do it in front of a mirror. Lovingly, forgive that person, for they knew not what disservice they were probably doing you.

When we look in the mirror, we're rarely well focused on what we're *saying* because we become hyperconscious of what we're *seeing*. Is **that** what my hair does when I turn my head? Do I look weird making that face? Did I have those lines next to my eyes last time I did this? Maybe if I speak standing slightly turned I'll look thinner...

Even if we like what we see in the mirror, it's a distraction and (here's the biggie), it's NOTHING like the experience of talking to an audience! No one will be staring back at you from three feet away. No one will be mimicking your every movement. No one will be blocking your view of the entire group. Of course it's a self-conscious feeling...it's completely unnatural!

Talk to a wall that is as far from you as you can manage indoors. If you're in your bedroom, stand over by the dresser and talk across the bed to the window. Even if that's only nine feet away, it's still more like being on stage than the mirror is. Then make "eye contact" with things on that wall while you're talking to simulate what you'd be doing on stage.

A patient pet can make a great audience for your speech rehearsal, no matter how many times you start over!

If you've got a pet, they make good audiences. They never critique and the topic never bores them. Though dogs may walk away... cats are probably more like most audience members. My cockatiel will stare at me about as long as I talk to her (if she were brighter, she might even be able to repeat sections).

And, of course, if you have a patient friend or partner, it's great to practice to them. You might even get useful feedback...if your relationship is strong enough to handle that!

2. Record for feedback.

So, having said all this about the mirror, it's not necessarily a bad thing to be able to critique your work...just not *while* you're doing it. I believe a great first step is to audio record yourself and play that back.

There's no lying to a tape recorder. There's no hiding behind facial expressions or graphics. Do you sound dynamic, interesting, clear, and concise? If not, it doesn't matter how great your outfit or handout is, you need to keep practicing how you sound.

Once you think it sounds okay (knowing fully well that it IS going to be better with visuals than just on tape), you can take the additional step of camcordering yourself. But by then, you'll have already worked out a pretty good auditory portion so you'll only be watching your gestures, facial expressions, and movement — not worrying about the words you use.

3. Write and memorize your opening!

It's acceptable to use notes and/or PowerPoint when you'll be talking for a while, but there's something about looking at notes in the first few minutes that is off-putting. It gives the impression that you have not prepared and that the session will be spent being read to.

Even if it's only a couple of minutes, have your opening comments, tales, statistics, etc. fully memorized so that you can be fully engaging and connected to your audience. It's your first chance to grab their attention so look ready and professional.

---

4. Write and memorize your stories!

Write them? What? But then they won't sound spontaneous, you cry out!

In a word, horse poop! Okay that's two words, but that's how strongly I feel about the matter. And this is coming from a professional improviser!

Doug Stevenson changed my mind about this issue in his speaker training program called StoryTheater. StoryTheater focuses on making our speeches more like performance to keep our audiences enthralled. When you meet Doug, you are instantly caught up in his exuberant energy and his natural way of telling stories. He can do this quite spontaneously, but he's the one who taught me *not* to do this in my stories on stage.

"I tell everyone to write down their best stories," Doug says. "Every word of it, as if it were going to be printed. It's only when you do that that you can look at it and say, 'Hmm...actually, the word tremendous would be stronger than huge. And I can see now how a couple of words here could save me several sentences later."

Writing out your stories also allow you to give yourself better feedback. Most of us are more accustomed to and skillful at critiquing writing than speaking. We can use our word processors to move things around and try them different ways.

When speakers are "forced" to go through this process, they are often amazed how much tighter and more vibrantly worded their stories can become.

Once you have it written just the perfect way, why would you ever want your audience to hear it as anything less? Your audience deserves to experience it as well as you can write it when you take the time to.

"But wait!" you cry out again. "The written word sounds so formal and stuffy compared to the way I speak. It won't sound good!"

Ah! If that's true, it's because you're writing like you're going to hand it in to a teacher for grading. If it doesn't sound natural when you read it aloud, change it! Let the words sound like your voice...just with the best possible words you could speak. If "words" like 'shoulda' or 'fantabulous' or 'oooo-ee' are natural for you, go back and put them in there where they belong!

And when it's just perfectly the way you would want to say it, start memorizing. When you have it so cold that it flows easier than the pledge of allegiance, THAT'S when you can decide, "Hmm, for this particular crowd, I think I know where I can stick in a line about ___ because they'll relate-to/take-interest-in/laugh-at that variation." Having your stories memorized gives you the power to do that effectively. Now you can think through the way you always do it so as to plan where to customize and "ad-lib" for this audience.

I've learned so much from Doug's work that I offer his books and great audio CDs about the StoryTheater process through my own website. The direct link is www.IMPROVentures.com/resources. They're fun and full of ideas that should align well with what you've been reading here.

5. At first, rehearse it with notes in hand.

Why work on memorizing something until you know that it's the way you like it? Give yourself a break and rehearse initially with the notes (or even the exact script) so that you get to hear the tone, feeling, humor and more without focusing on having it committed to memory yet.

You're less likely to like what you're coming up with if you're trying to work on remembering it AND learning to deliver it well at the same time.

6. **Second, begin working sections from memory, letting go of how good you deliver for now.**

Once you move into memorization, treat that like a new stage of the game. Give yourself permission to deliver it stiffly with as many awkward pauses as you need to remember what comes next.

Take small a small chunk to work on getting down cold before looking at the next one.

---

7. **Third, make that little section sound good.**

Go back and work on making that little section sound as good as it did when you were reading it. Do it until you've almost got it to the confidence level that you hope to deliver on D-Day.

When you can do it well (note: I didn't say perfectly), go back to step 6 and take on the next chunk.

When you can do three chunks well, try to do all three without stopping. When you can do that well (and it might take a few tries now that there's so much), you can go back for chunks four, five, and six in the same way.

---

8. **Fifth, add the pizzazz.**

When you're doing okay with the material and knowing what comes next isn't the challenge anymore, rehearse some more: this time, trying ideas for body movement, props, humor, better quick reference stories, and possibly interaction.

This is taking your good speech and making it lively and more captivating.

---

9. Practice on your feet whenever possible.

Part of what practice is about is, as much as possible, creating the experience for yourself in advance. If you don't plan on speaking from a chair, don't rehearse it that way.

Every gesture...every head turn...every body move done in a chair feels different when standing. As discussed in point number 1, even from your very first reading of your material, stand and talk to the furthest possible wall when you are rehearsing. If that means taking breaks to get off your feet, so be it.

---

10. JUST DO IT!!!

If there's a professional speaker out there who loves rehearsing, I haven't met him yet. It's not all glamour and praise; it's a job with work to be done. This is a big part of the work.

I go to the gym even on the days I REALLY don't want to be there. If I only lift for ten minutes and then want to leave, I can. But I've kept lifting in my life for that day and every little bit helps. Same with rehearsal. Even if you think you can only stomach ten minutes of it, do it!!! You'll improve a little in those ten minutes and, more than likely, you'll actually do twenty once you get started.

One of the keys for me is to be sure I have time and space for myself. If anyone else is around, I get self-conscious and can't truly articulate with oomph. Create a safe space to be silly, fallible, and focused.

"Oh, Milo," my reading audience cries. "You make it sound so simple, but I'm terrible at memorization! I just can't do it!"

Yeah, yeah, yeah...my coaching clients have said that, too. It *is* easier for some than others, but we *all* can do it. Sounds like a topic for a chapter unto itself...

17

10 Cool Tricks to Ease the Torture of Memorization

No question, this is the number two problem that I hear...just behind generalized "fear". Unless you're extremely fortunate or gifted, memorization takes work. But there *are* things you can do to take the sting out of it, especially if you are creating your own program.

1. **Write like you talk.**

One thing I notice clients do is to write more formally than they speak. Writing formally has its place, but it's mostly for when the words are going to be read ON the page by someone else...not OFF the page by you!

While one might write a sentence like:

"I do not believe that we are all alone in this large world that we share."

But would you ever really talk like that? Wouldn't it be more likely to come out as:

"I don't believe we're all alone in this big world of ours."

> *Our time investment with clientele yielded heightened returns in the tertiary quartile.*
>
> *Dang...just say 3rd quarter sales are up!*

Write for speaking in a way that sounds like you'd actually talk.

Try saying each of those sentences and, unless you're in line for the throne of England, you'll find that latter is not only more *natural* to say, but allows for the addition of your natural *inflections* on words like "all" or "alone".

Next, forget what Mrs. Horowitz said about your paragraph structure in the fifth grade. You hit that carriage return any time there's a new thought or a break in logic chunks. If you are going to use a phrase like "smart as a bug in a rug", make sure it all appears on the same line, even if you have to leave half a line blank to do so. Who cares? This isn't for Mrs. Horowitz...it's for you! Keeping logic together really helps.

Allow your paragraphs to be shorter than you would for an essay. Have you noticed that I'm doing this throughout this book? Longer paragraphs, like the one above this one, tire the mind during processing. And if you think that's true for reading, well, kiddo, it's twice as bad for memorizing!

So write like you talk and memorizing it will be easier.

---

2. Take tiny bites, not gorging ones.

I heard a famous TV actress say one time that the only way she could get through a weekly script was to do one page at a time and not even look at the next page until she could do that page solidly. Then she'd work on her second page until that was okay.

This method keeps the amount you're trying to digest from being overwhelming. Since there's no dialogue to give you a moment to think, the bite you take might be as small as five lines.

I recommend a three tier approach. Decide what size bite you can handle. Get it close to memorized. Move on to the next. Memorize it. Repeat for a third time. Now try to run through all three. Work that until you can do it. THEN start again for bites 4-6. Then 7-9.

Only try to get through all of 1-9 after succeeding at this. It may take you a while because you'll forget 1-3 by now, but look how far you've come...you're working on 1-9 and it seems doable!

By the time you approach bite #10, you'll have had some real success behind you.

---

3. Don't memorize anything that could make a great visual or which makes sense to read!

Let your PowerPoint take care of as much as it can so you don't have to memorize as much. If you have five points, let PowerPoint reflect them. If you need to list seven famous women who never married, don't memorize the list...put up those seven faces with their names underneath each.

Remember: Any time you can add visuals, you're also making your program more appealing, so don't hold back when those visuals can help YOU!

---

4. Record the audio of your speech.

Note that I didn't say video; this isn't about critiquing technique...it's about memorization. Audio-record yourself and then recite along with it. It'll prompt you if you forget and you can rewind until speaking along with it becomes natural.

When you make this recording, be sure to be reading it exactly from paper with inflections as you like them so that you're certain to be audio-studying from the right words.

You may decide as you speak along with the tape that you'd like to change a word or phrase here and there. Great! You wouldn't have realized it otherwise. Just speak the better words over the other one for that moment until you can re-record.

The technology keeps changing. It used to be easy to record onto a cassette and play it in my car for study on the go. Now I have to either record on a special digital recording device OR record on my computer mike, transfer it to MP3, load that into my mp3 player, and broadcast that via a converter to an FM station on my car radio. Yeesh...hooray for technology!

---

5. Use activity time to your advantage.

One of my greatest discoveries in including audience activities is that it takes all the focus off me for a few moments! This allows me to look at my notes, check my pacing, sip some tea, etc.

The more you get them doing, the less you have to memorize and the more you break down your program into manageable chunks for memorization.

6.   Keyword sheet instead of notes.

Full sentence notes can be too cumbersome to find your place in quickly. A *keyword sheet* is a better approach. It is similar to an outline, but more useful in this case.

After outlining and scripting your speech, go backwards and create a keyword sheet to hit the concepts you need to cover. Here's an example, a section from a client's speech that we recently worked on together. Note the words that I underlined:

> "<u>I have kids</u> now and my greatest prayer is that somehow they inherited all of their <u>genes...from their mother</u>. Because I don't know if I can take raising a child like I was. <u>My parents</u>, being highly-educated and academically-brilliant people, an orthopedic surgeon and a respected clinical psychologist, sent their only son to <u>private school</u> through 4th grade so he'd do as well or better than them. I'm still <u>not sure why</u> private school was supposed to be better for me...but somehow, <u>what I learned</u>...was how <u>to screw around</u>. Make people laugh. Work the teacher's last nerve. Pull off brilliant practical jokes that <u>the principal</u> *never* saw the humor in...no matter how well we got to know each other <u>after school</u>."

All of these lines get turned into the following on a keyword sheet:

> I have kids...genes from mother
> My parents...private school...not sure why
> What I learned...to screw around
> the principal...after school."

Does it have the detail of the first script? No, but he's supposed to be rehearsing so that he knows what he wants to say about each point. The keyword sheet just helps him to remember what point is working up to next.

Ideally, rehearsing with just the keyword sheet instead of paragraphs, he'll eventually not need the keyword sheet either. But if he does, look how much simpler that is than following lines of text.

Keyword sheets, if used on stage, can be on index cards for easier holding than paper. And, of course, if you *are* going to stand behind the lectern the whole time, it's still a better resource on one or two sheets of paper than pages and pages of an entire script.

7. Plan to use what you've seen in the room

This one takes a little planning and you have to remember to follow through, but it's effective. Plan to refer to something in the room which you can talk about without having to memorize it.

This can be implemented in as many ways as you can be creative with so it's a bit challenging to tell you how best to apply it. Suppose, for instance, you are talking about different pets people have. Instead of memorizing national statistics, count off the first twenty people you see (i.e.: the first two rows of eight and four more in the next row). Do a quick census on the board of how many have dogs, cats, etc. Ask if there are any pets you've forgotten.

All of this gives you a sample chart to refer to, creates some interaction, opens the door to adlibs for humor (like the lady who has a rat or the guy with the potbelly pig is bound to be good for a few fun references). If it reflects national data, great! If not, you can say that too, without having to remember it precisely.

---

8. Use memory tricks for association.

For me, associations are usually the best way to remember what comes next. And the sillier, the better!

Let's go back to my client in the earlier example trying to memorize a section from his keyword sheet:

> I have kids...genes from mother
> My parents...private school...I learned to screw around

First, I'd picture a kid in those ridiculously-tight Jordache jeans we wore in the early 1980s. Why jeans? Because I'm trying to connect the words 'Kid' and 'Genes'. Why tight 1980s Jordaches? Because it's a more specific, outlandish and playful image than a kid in an ordinary pair of Levi's. Could I have chosen super-baggy jeans or ones with something embroidered butterflies on it? Sure...whatever works to make it a distinctly strong image.

Now I've gotten from 'kids' to 'genes from mother'. 'Mother' to 'My Parents' is so easy that I don't need a memory trick.

I then picture my parents as adults, dressed in little prep school uniforms, sitting in a class surrounded by 25 fourth graders in the same outfit, looking oddly at the two grown ups squeezed into the little desks. Does this sound ludicrous? It is! But it's extremely memorable and that's what we're looking for.

Finally, I picture a fancy private school with a giant, King-Kong-sized, Phillips-head screw sitting on top of the roof, holding the school together. Totally absurd.

But now notice just how easy it is to memorize his keyword sheet. Kids...jeans/genes...mother...my parents...private school...screw around.

Maybe I'm certifiable, but I'll take that over having patchy hair from ripping it out in frustration as I try to memorize everything in the perfect sentence structure that Mrs. Horowitz valued so highly.

---

9.   Cheat!

Again, Mrs. Horowitz isn't here, looking over the end-of-the-nose-glasses. There are little things you can do to cheat and if it makes you better, it can only be a good thing.

Remember point number 10 on the list **"10 Smart Ways to Maximize Your PowerPoint Experience"**. In that list, I explained how I got creative in having PowerPoint prompt me for the next thing I needed to say. Be creative like that for yourself!

Another time, in a small room, I had an ally post up a keyword sheet on the back wall after everyone else had sat down. No one knew I was glancing at it now and then.

Yet another time, I posted my keyword sheet on the side of the lectern. I had to turn it slightly so that only I would see it, but it worked!

Here's another PowerPoint cheat that I love: I couldn't remember what story came after the one about my father's paddleball game. The lesson of the story showed up as words on the screen, but I kept blanking as to what came next, which was a story about the company 3M.

So what did I do? I found a sports image to put underneath the moral of my Dad's story. It was an illustration (just one that came with the PowerPoint software) showing a bunch of runners in a race. Then I put numbers on the runners. One of the runners "numbers" was 3M. That picture now ALWAYS reminds me of what's coming next without being a distraction at all. In fact, I've asked a few people; none had noticed that the runner even had a number on his vest.

Mrs. Horowitz would have said, "When you cheat someone else, you cheat yourself." But when it hurts no one and helps you, cheat!

---

10. Done with a smile, the audience will forgive you for going over to your notes.

The audience wants you to be enjoyable, on-target and clear; they aren't looking for infallibility. It's okay to occasionally head back to them. The trick is to never look flustered by it, so the audience doesn't feel uncomfortable about it.

For instance, this would be an example of it being well handled:

"And the three factors in the equation for fire are fuel, heat, and...hmm...hang on a second...(checking notes)...ah, of course, oxygen. Something I apparently lacked to my brain for a second. (smile)"

A gentle moment of humanity that will make the audience warm up to you and you move on. No big deal.

Great! So now it's more believable that you could memorize material and deliver it for a while without straining your brain to do it. But are you sure you could do it without straining your *voice*? Especially if you were speaking all day (either on stage or in and out of meetings)? Let's take a look at how to protect your most powerful speaking resource!

18

10 Insiders Secrets for the Best Use of Your Voice

I've been at this long enough and attended enough speaking seminars that I could probably do a decent job on this topic, but I thought I'd let an expert take this on, as long as I happen to have access to a great one...who was willing!

Joni Wilson is an internationally known voice trainer and performance coach. She is the creator of the amazing 3-Dimensional Voice™ Technique and author of the Wilson Voice Series. The first book in this series (The 3-Dimensional Voice: Fun and Easy Method of Voice Improvement) was a #1 best-seller for months on amazon.com in the category of "Voice and Public Speaking".

I'm thrilled to be turning this chapter over to Joni for her words of wisdom, so if it doesn't sound like me, now you'll know why!

Thanks, Milo! Hi, everyone — Joni Wilson here. The voice is an effective tool we humans use to communicate with each other. We can voice the same words in different combinations and create amazing poetry, song lyrics or one-line zingers. A few badly chosen words in the wrong combination can start a war, while a few well-chosen words masterfully woven together can bring peace. Words can be as sharp as a sword and wound just as deeply and yet sometimes saying just one little word can make the heart leap for joy and completely change a life.

As speakers, a good voice is vital to every ear that hears our brilliant, well-chosen words. So many people give countless hours to their organization of material and to practicing their technique...only to undermine the entire performance by working with a voice that is not working at its best.

I'm happy to share a few insider secrets for protecting your voice and I'm glad Milo chose to include this as a chapter topic. Here are ten facts every speaker should know about his/her voice. Drill them deep into your brain until they become part of your belief system because... The voice has no brain of its own and only believes what you believe!

---

1.   **You can't cheat on this.**

No quick vocal fix is ever a substitute for good voice technique. If you choose to abuse your voice, some things will reflect immediately and others will slowly get worse over time, but either way, it will take its toll.

If anyone tells you, "Voice rest will solve your vocal problems," don't believe them! Vocal problems are caused by overuse and abuse of the vocal cords. You can rest them, but if you do not learn how to use them correctly, the problem will always return!

---

2.   **Avoid whispering.**

Never whisper if you are losing your voice. The whispering effect will further damage the cords. Use a pad and write notes if you have to communicate at a time when talking hurts or when you are protecting your voice for a necessary use later.

---

3.   **Mind the air.**

Excessive heat and air-conditioning affect the voice by dehydrating the vocal cords. Turn them both OFF when you are sleeping, especially when traveling., and especially if speaking early in the morning afterward.

4. **Nix the "A-hems".**

Do not clear your throat with a vengeance. Excessive throat clearing is a habit. The more you try to clear it, the more mucous will be created to protect your vocal cords. It is a never-ending battle and you cannot win it. Try sipping water to move the larynx into a lowered relax position.

If accessing water is not an option in the moment and clearing your throat feels essential, make the gentlest cough you can; it's almost like a cross between a "H" and "K". It can even be done with the mouth closed for less sound. It's not a perfect solution, but it will accomplish about as much as a traditional throat clearing, is gentler on the voice box, and makes less noise.

Sip room temperature water as a better option than the counter-productive throat clearing.

5. Just say no to Ricola.

Never use cough drops with menthol if you are speaking. The temptation is strong because it feels so good, but what you are doing is numbing so that you cannot feel any damage you are doing!

The cooling factor in menthol freezes the vocal cords. You want them warm and plumped, not cold and shrunken. If you need a quick soothing feeling, lemon drops are a great way to produce saliva, which is just what your throat wants.

---

6. Pass up the ice water.

Every business meeting seems to provide ice water to appease everyone inexpensively. If you think menthol will freeze your throat, that's NOTHING compared to what iced drinks will do!

The best temperature for drinks before and during speaking is in the range between room temperature and comfortably hot. There's no advantage in burning your throat, but tea that's on the border of warm and hot can be very nice.

In particular, there's an excellent tea made by Traditional Medicines called "Throat Coat" (available in many supermarkets, drug stores, and health food markets). The ingredients in Throat Coat are very soothing without masking symptoms.

---

7. Save the Sudafed and Dristan for afterward.

If you catch a cold and have to use your voice, do not take decongestants. Their job is to dry up mucous no matter where it lives in the body. Your vocal cords live in mucous. If you dry it up, the voice will sound rough and scratchy.

As an added factor, antihistamines make many people sleepy at a time when they'll be summoning all possible energy to be lively!

If you need something to get you through, Traditional Medicines also makes a wonderful tea called "Breathe Easy" which seems to open passages while giving your throat a warm, soothing bath. (I don't have stock in Traditional Medicines teas, by the way; they just make good products.)

---

8. Breathe deep, even if you have to slow down to do it.

The vocal cords work like valves and need a strong supply of compressed air to perform their magic! Keep pumping that air. If you don't give the voice box the air it needs to project, you'll either be too soft or strain to reach your volume.

Imagine your rib cage expanding to take in all the air, rather than filling your chest. Then, plant yourself strongly on both feet and imagine pushing downward toward the ground with the muscles in your belly to force the air out of your throat and mouth.

That's what you see the stars on talent shows like "American Idol" doing to get those final long notes out; they know the trick!

---

9. Say AHHHHHHHHH.

The voice is acoustic and needs space. Trying to project with a half open mouth is like trying to blow out all the candles on a cake through a drinking straw...there's just not enough room for it to work.

For your words to be heard in the back of the room your mouth must be OPEN!

---

10. Find the cause of any problems you have.

Though some people are born like Ethel Merman, ready to project across a field, almost everyone is capable of a good, strong, effective voice.

A weak voice is only the effect. To strengthen it, you must find the cause, which is a topic beyond a little ten point list. But it can be done and I encourage you to learn how!

My thanks to Joni for taking on this task, which I hope you found useful. She's helped me immensely as a coach on this issue. For more information on Joni and her books, audio-CDs, and coaching, visit:

> www.JoniWilsonVoice.com

At long last, the issue that brings most of my clients to me...or at least they THINK it's their biggest issue: FEAR!

Given that the terms "Public Speaking" and "Fear" are almost synonymous for some people, I thought we deserved a whole chapter on the topic.

19

10 Healing Ways to Deal With the FEAR and Reduce the STRESS

When people come to me for coaching, they list their concerns on a survey they fill out upon arriving. Although it isn't always the top reason, the most commonly checked box is "getting over the fear around speaking". On occasion, it's the only box checked!

I'm not sure why people who will bungee jump at the drop of a hat can be unnerved by looking at twenty faces and speaking to them, but I can't deny how common the feeling is.

When my clients and I talk about the fear of speaking, I tell them that there are two dimensions to the fear: *reality-based fear* and *created fear*.

Reality-based fears are those things that can cause fear because they reflect the situation. Is your opening poorly written? I can see why it would make you nervous to have to deliver that, then. Did you spend only ten minutes trying to commit eight pages to memory? Yes, you have reason to believe you might flounder if you try to do it without notes.

"Created fear" expends energy on things that are truly unlikely.

The other kind of fear is what I call **created fear**. It's stress where the same circumstances could create fear in one person but not another. For instance, we are creating fear if we worry if we might fall off the stage when there's not a logical reason in the world that that should happen to us when it never has before. Created fear is our brain working overtime and there are things we can do to minimize this.

Both kinds of fear are valid and need to be dealt with, but the solutions to each are different.

Reality-based fear is dealt with by changing as many of the circumstances as you can. That's what the first three-quarters of this book have been about. No matter how scary the general, created fear of speaking can be, I don't know many people who would be *equally* afraid about an event for which they had prepared and another for which they hadn't.

For most people I work with, the vast majority of their fear is coming from them knowing that they aren't as organized, rehearsed, and polished as they should be. This fear is only reduced by good work up front. I've had clients tell me that, in spite of originally listing "fear" as a giant concern, it had mostly abated by the "big day" because they felt so well prepared. So, we deal with the *causes* of reality-based fear first before even trying to help ourselves deal with the stuff we're conjuring up.

That said, there's a very human response to stimulus that will cause some stress no matter how prepared you are. The one that says, "What if I forget what comes next? What if the PowerPoint projector overheats? What if my boss falls asleep during my presentation?"

Once we've done all that we can to arrive prepared, here are some things we can to deal with the stress itself to reduce fear further.

---

1. **Get some perspective.**

Ask yourself, out loud if you're alone, "Is this thing I fear really going to affect my survival?" After all, there's no greater risk than survival. Much as we throw around phrases like, "I could have died" or "That comedian really died up there", to my knowledge no one has ever actually died from giving a poor speech.

So survival isn't at risk. Then work your way back from there. Will anything happen to your family and close friends if the speech goes awry? No? Will it affect your home life? No? Will you lose your job? Even if it doesn't reflect positively, almost never will you lose your job! Will you get demoted? Again, highly unlikely.

Keep going, working your way back to truly what is the worst thing that could happen if problems occur and that perspective can be very relaxing.

Realistically, in most cases, the worst that will happen is that a few people in the audience might get a little bored or feel bad for you if you flounder. That's hardly the end of the world.

---

2. Acknowledge and define the fear.

Get to the bottom of it so it isn't so big. I'm scared of "this" is too big for your brain to process, so make it smaller. Are you:

- Afraid of someone(s) in particular there?
- Afraid of the technology you'll be using?
- Afraid of losing your place?
- Afraid of tripping over the words?
- Afraid of forgetting what comes next?
- Afraid of questions you can't answer?

The list goes on. Unless you're like Charlie Brown at Lucy's 5¢ Psychiatry booth...

Lucy: How about pantaphobia, Charlie Brown? Do you think you might have pantaphobia?
CB: What's that?
Lucy: The fear of everything.
CB: (screaming and blowing her away) THAT'S IT!!!

...odds are not every aspect of the day is probably scary. For instance, maybe you are afraid of losing your place and forgetting what comes next, but Q&A is easy for you and there will be no one in the room you are intimidated by. In fact, saying No to that last option might remind you of the support you have there.

The simple act of saying Yes to some and No to others brings clarity and, surprisingly, a bit of peace because you can start moving created fears into reality-based ones and look at strategies for minimizing them.

With each option you come up with and say No or even Not-Really to (like the falling off the stage one), you remind yourself of what's real and what you can let go of.

---

3. Mental rehearsal.

In a place where you'll have quiet and no interruptions, sit comfortably and close your eyes. For several minutes (at least five; don't rush it), imagine yourself going through the process with everything going right.

Imagine the room set up perfectly. Picture the person introducing you sounding eager to hear from you. Visualize the audience smiling as you begin. Hear them laughing when you hit humorous lines. See them nodding as you hit poignant moments. Enjoy the creation of them clapping enthusiastically afterward. Add in the details that are specific for your group.

First, your subconscious holds this image and treats it like reality, so it's a calming experience. The more you repeat the exercise, the more clearly it rests in your subconscious.

On the actual day, as some of those things prove to be true, the imaging you did is reinforced. With each reinforced image, the calm you felt while picturing it all makes more sense to your subconscious and your body gets the signal that all is well. And you relax...possibly in spite of your created fears attempts to create more stress.

---

4. Talk about your fear with someone who cares about you.

Obvious as this may seem, many of us feel we should be able to pull ourselves up by the bootstraps and handle this. We might even try to dismiss the fear, thinking, "This is stupid. I don't know what I'm so afraid of, so it would sound dumb to try to talk this out." Logical or not, keeping it inside gives the created fear a total playground to drive you nuts.

Ask a friend if you can have a couple of minutes just to vent about the fear around this. Let them know you don't need solutions and will be happy if they just listen, but that you're open to their thoughts, too. You may get a great relief in talking freely about it in more than a sentence...especially if that sentence is "I'm scared about Friday." The more you say that, the more your subconscious hears it as something 100% reality based when that's unlikely the case.

---

5. Step outside yourself when the voices start.

When the demons start up in your head, step *outside* the noise and say to yourself, "Oh, that's just that annoying fear that my brain is using to try to protect me. Thank you for doing your job, Brain, but I'm fine without those thoughts."

While it may sound nutty, it's a great exercise to train yourself that we are NOT the product of our thoughts. We are the product of the thoughts we choose to *accept, acknowledge, and act upon.*

If it helps and feels appropriate, another variation on this is to look at the source. Whose message to you is this really? Is it a negative message Mom gave you? Or a teacher? Or someone else? If so, direct the response to them:

"Thanks, Mom, for sending me the usual message. I know that's your way of trying to protect me but I'm going to choose to think another way."

Oh, and let's be clear: You say this to your mother in your *head*; not via AT&T!

---

6. Use practice as your response instead of panic.

You can also respond by practicing something in your program. Instead of dwelling on the "what if I forget what comes next?" fear, respond by taking 2-3 minutes to go over one little section and prove to yourself that you're doing fine. Your subconscious gets the message "capable" instead of "scared".

7. **Engage in some physical activity.**

Stress is cyclical:

    a. Your mind produces it
    b. Your body stores it.
    c. Your mind notices that your body seems stressed.
    d. Your mind is stressed by this realization.
    e. Repeat until driven insane.

We can break this cycle with exercise, the most natural way to reduce physical stress. While half an hour on the treadmill can do wonders, you can still reap the benefits of exercise on a far smaller scale. Even walking twice around the office building, especially while thinking about something pleasant can break the cycle and you'll feel better.

Making room for exercise in your life will keep stress down on many levels and boost your endorphins (the natural feel-good chemical in your body) that will have you feeling good on many levels.

8. **"Fake it till you make it."**

Pretend that you are courageous and confident and you will experience a surge in these feelings. Our brains don't always recognize when we are lying to it.

Saying things to yourself like "Woo-hoo! That practice was fun and I'm getting better!" make an impact on our stress levels, even if we're not quite sure we believe them.

The tricky part is that you can't follow that thought with a sarcastic, "Yeah, right...sure I am...yeesh..."

9. **Use signs.**

Earlier, I mentioned using signs to help you remember. You can also use them to help you relax.

Put two signs where only you will see them from the stage, preferably not near each other. Put "SMILE! ☺" on one and "BREATHE" on the other. When you notice one of them, do what it says.

Too self-conscious to have actual signs? Add two clipart characters to your PowerPoint, say a duck and a puppy. Name the duck "Smile" and the puppy "Breathe". Any time you see the character, do what his name says. Only you will know this is happening.

You can use characters or symbols on signs as well so that only you know what they mean. If one sign said, "Welcome!" (which you know means smile) and the other said "Relax!" (which you know means breathe), who would know you put the signs up for anyone but them?

Having said all this, when you smile, your audience is more likely to. When you breathe, your audience is more likely to. Seeing either of these has an effect of relaxing you.

---

10. **Remember the reason you are there.**

This one is simple, yet very real. 99% of the time, this is not a contest. This is not a test of your speaking skills. This is not a judgment session. You are there for a *purpose*; it's not about you. It's about the message you are there to deliver and you are just a vehicle for it. In the long run, all of your nerves are about your ego and they have nothing to do with what the people in the room are coming for.

They are almost always looking for content. They'll appreciate, retain, and implement it more often if it's well delivered, but in the end, it's the message they are coming for.

Remembering the following sentence; it can be helpful in calming yourself by setting reasonable expectations:

"Serve the message and you have served your audience."

Do just that and you've already earned a "B". And remember that a "B" means "above average" so that really is a good place to be.

I hope with these ideas you can relax enough to bring your well-prepared program to the stage with a calm mind and body.

Once you've relaxed enough to deliver your program confidently, you're all done and ready to go home and relax. Or are you? A great many programs, especially smaller ones, will end with a Question & Answer period. Didn't they listen? Haven't you said everything they need to know? Rarely. People will often have specifics that you hadn't thought to include or a specific incident they'd like your input on. And others just want to show off what they know. Any way you look at it, Q&A is a part of most programs so it's worth discussing strategies for it.

20
10 Ideas for Dealing with Q&A

Q&A is a place where some people shine because they can show how well they speak off the cuff on a topic. For others, that's just what makes this the worst part of it all.

Ideally, this time should showcase that you really know your stuff …you can handle this topic even beyond what you've prepared.

Here are some ideas to tackle the Q&A time successfully.

1. Don't make it the last thing you do.

This point surprises some people who have always assumed that it *has* to be. Just another time in life to which we can say, "Why?" since it's not in our best interest.

You're probably going to come up with a nice conclusion to end on a pleasant, professional note. Why sacrifice that to ending on Q&A which can be a little disjointed, is not fully in your control, and feels like a clunky place to stop?

Q&A doesn't have to be all at once. You can designate two or three points for Q&A, though it's nice to include the caveat, "Any questions up to this point?" so that you can politely reply, if needed, "Great question. I'll be getting to that."

2. **Decide in advance how you will schedule questions.**

Try to arrange Q&A to be *second-to-last* and end with your conclusion. This is easily accomplished by saying some variation on: "Before I do my conclusion, I'd like to open up the floor for about five minutes for questions, if there are any."

If questions are fewer than you expected, you finish just a bit early or can expand a bit on your conclusion, but at least you know it before you end. That's a lot better than ending on that cavern of empty sound after "Any questions…no?…ok, um, well…thanks."

If there are more questions than expected, leave just enough time for how long your conclusion will be.

---

3. **Have a good story ready as filler.**

It's quite possible that the same presentation that yielded a dozen questions for one group may raise only one or even no questions with another audience.

After taking a good (albeit painfully long) five seconds to see if a hand finally goes up, it's nice to have something *planned* to say to fill the silence and a bit of the extra time. Have a little story ready that expands on something you said earlier. Or be ready with, "While you're thinking, one of the questions I sometimes get is…"

When the audience sees that questions are so few that you are filler-talking, someone *might* respond after your extra story after you prompt them with "One last chance to share a question?"

---

4. **Show interest and compliment questions.**

Eye-contact, nodding and/or smiling during questions is very appropriate to show interest. It's nice to follow up with something like:

"Great question."
"Interesting..."
"I'm glad someone brought that up."

All of these make you seem approachable and make it easier for the next person to raise their hand.

I used "I'm glad you asked about that" with a big smile one time when a man's question was the last thing in the world I wanted him to ask about. But it immediately diffused the notion that I was trying to hide something. By answering his question eagerly and as best I could, I came off as well I could have under the circumstances.

Seem glad to get the question, even if you're not particularly. Talk and look primarily at the questioner, but break to look at the whole audience to include them, too.

---

5. Make sure everyone knows the question.

No one wants to feel like they missed the question that was not on microphone. If there are more than 15 people in the room, repeat the question verbatim before answering it, as in:

"Good point *(note my use of compliment)*. The question she asked was: 'What can we do when a client brings up our competition's prices?' The first thing I like to do is..."

While it may seem like it would be enough to restate the question in the answer, as in:

"When the client brings up our competition's prices, what I like to do first is..."

the problem is that YOU know you restated the question, but the audience may not and part of their brains are focused on figuring if they got the question right

For smaller groups, restate the question within the answer (just in case someone daydreamed) is fine because everyone should have been able to hear the question.

6. **Consider having a "plant".**

If you can get over the idea that this feels deceptive, it's a really nice way to include information that didn't have an exact fit to your program.

Have someone (it can even be a key figure from their group) ask a question you'd like to answer.

Since the question and the answer will go well, it also puts others at ease that Q&A is a good thing.

That's not a small thing. I'm pretty bold, but I recall a high school teacher I had who responded so harshly to our questions that by November, no one would ask anything...no matter how confused they were! I don't expect you're like that, but make an effort to be the distinct opposite.

7. **Try to be brief.**

It's just a question, not another speech on a new topic. Try to keep your answers simple and on target, especially if there are many hands going up or if the question seems to be of a personal interest and not one the whole group will benefit from.

8. **Use available methods to defer questions.**

Not every question can or should be answered in this setting:

- You may not have the data for the answer memorized.
- The question might be outside the scope of the event you are speaking at.
- The question may be inappropriate.
- The answer, even if accurate, might not be appropriate coming from you instead of the person who should be answering it.
- You might not have a clue what the answer is.

Find a polite way to excuse yourself from answering irrelevant or uncomfortable questions, including offering to speak to that person later. This must be done in a friendly, helpful way, of course, rather than making them feel as though answering to would be a bother:

> "Interesting question...and more than I can go into in this setting. Would you be willing to approach me after the session or give me a call so I can talk to you later about this?"

rather than:

> "That's more than I can talk about here. You can call me later if you really need an answer on that."

If the answers aren't readily available but you could answer later, refer them to a website or your email for more information.

When you don't know the answer at all, admit that you don't know rather than faking it. Ask who *else* might be able to answer this question. If the person is present, ask if they would address the issue briefly. If they are not in attendance, you can point out that it's worth contacting him later. Make it clear that you wish you could discuss their thoughts further, but it's just outside the scope of what you feel qualified to discuss.

A nice thing to add in this case is, "If you find out the answer to that, would you drop me an email so I'll know in case I'm ever asked again?" This really honors their question, empowers them to move forward from the knowledge you shared, makes you more memorable to them, and could even yield you valuable info.

---

9. Consider getting questions in advance.

For larger audiences, getting questions in advance can be a great idea. It allows you to looking through them in advance and answer as many as time permits, choosing the ones that you'd most like to answer.

This is accomplished by telling the meeting planner that you plan to take this approach and creating a means by which people can submit questions to you via email, a webpage, or on index cards that they can bring to the meeting and drop off in a pre-determined location.

The only possible disadvantage to the index card option is that you don't get to see them before the day of the event. This may or may not matter to you.

...next, Lila Spencer in our I.T. Department asks...

Getting questions in advance can yield better questions and cut your stress.

10.   Skip it.

Truth be told, I think Q&A is usually overrated. Certain topics lend themselves to it better than others. Most of the time, five more minutes of well-written material is more valuable than five minutes of Q&A, so long as people know they can approach or contact you afterward.

If you'd rather not do it, ask the meeting planner if they have strong feelings about it. Most of the time, you'll find they'll say, "Do whatever you think is best." If they say they really want it, you're no worse off for having asked.

We mentioned in this section that having fewer questions than expected at Q&A can affect your pacing for your timeslot. Pacing is a critical aspect of your whole program, not just Q&A.

Let's spend some time on tips and tricks to make sure you pace your time well so you aren't rushing at the end or wondering how to fill the last ten minutes!

21

10 Crucial Techniques for Pacing Time

It's a terrible feeling to look at the clock and say to yourself, "Cripes! I've only covered half my material and I've used up two-thirds of my time!" (and maybe "Cripes!" isn't the kind of word that would come to mind.) Meeting planners have rated "running over time" as one of the most terrible problems a speaker can cause...no matter how good the rest of their program was!

Likewise, one does not want to realize later that he barreled through the first half of his material in only twenty minutes and he still has forty minutes of speaking time remaining.

I used to think it was amazing that *anyone* could ever really know that their program would last exactly an hour or exactly two hours. Now I realize that it's neither magic nor luck...it's a combination of good planning and improvisation.

The trick is to be so good at it that it looks effortless. Let's take a look at some things you can do to set yourself up for success in pacing.

1. **Find out in advance if the ending time is absolute or if it's fine to run over.**

"Milo, darling, you'll be on from 1pm to 2pm. Is that okay?"

"That sounds great, Millie, but just so I know...as I'm pacing myself, sometimes the program looks to be headed to 65 minutes instead of 60. If that's what I see, I can *absolutely* make sure it ends on time if you need me to OR I can finish in 65. Is there anything going on afterward such that finishing precisely by two o'clock is necessary?

She'll either say:

> "2...2:05...what's the difference? Finish when it feels done."

or:

> "No, the next activity really needs to start at 2, so be sure to finish on time."

Either way, make it sound like what she replied is great and that you just wanted to check for her sake.

---

2. **If they start you late, ask if they still want the whole presentation or if they want you to end on time.**

This is different than asking well in advance:

"Millie, I know we discussed me finishing right on time by 2pm, but things have clearly gotten a bit backed up and it looks like I'll be on more like 1:15 now. Would you like me to shorten my program to only 45 minutes so you're back on track or do you still want me to do my whole program, even though it will end at 2:15?"

Whatever she says, do! But at least now it's been her decision, not yours, so you are helping her reach her goal.

When this has come up in my speaking career, it's been pretty 50/50 what the response will be and sometimes the answer surprised me, so always ask.

---

3. **Find out if Q&A if optional.**

We mentioned this in the Q&A section, but it bears repeating that cutting, extending, or adding an unintended Q&A section could make all the difference in making your timing fit perfectly. This is especially true if the client never mentioned one way or the other if a Q&A section would be included.

---

4.   Rehearse for time.

Rehearse the whole piece, preferably with notes, so you know how long it takes under ideal circumstances. Then come to a decision of how much more time you think it will take live. Factors include:

- Your introduction
- Laughter time
- Interactive time (including getting their attention back)
- Any announcements

You may surprise yourself with how long or short it is to actually run it from beginning to end. It's easy to be interrupted when working that long so either put yourself in a setting where *nothing* can interrupt you OR have a stop watch you can pause during interruptions and mark exactly where you left off.

---

5.   Be prepared for announcements.

Announcements are just another thing that can unexpectedly take time you counted on. Make sure in advance that when they say you're on from 1 to 2pm, that's really *all* going to be your time (minus your introduction, which you've accounted for).

If they say, "Well, we'll make a few announcements in that time first...", you plan around that and expect only 50-55 minutes of speaking!

---

6.   **Choose a timepiece.**

Make a decision of what kind of timepiece will work best for you; then, bring it yourself. Never count on the room having what you'll need. Some rooms are purposely set up without them so attendees won't keep looking at it. It's a nice thought, but doesn't help you one bit!

If it's a clock, make it big enough and something you can stand up easily. I know some people who stand them on the lectern sideways so they can see them but the audience can't. I know others who have found clocks that have a flat base and stand them up between the stage and the front row. Whatever works best for you.

A colleague in the National Speakers Association likes to use a digital kitchen countdown timer with big numbers...and snips the wire to the speaker so there's no beeps or rings. Great idea!

---

7.   **Ask for a timekeeper with signals.**

One very common method is to set up a pre-determined person in the front row with reminder cards. You can decide for yourself what prompts you'd like them to signal.

For a one-hour program, I prefer minute signals at 20, 30, 40, 50, and 55. Some also like "Times Up", but I have a pretty good sense of what five minutes is and if I go 30 seconds over, no one cares...but it makes me feel tense to see that "Times Up" card sitting there during that last half minute.

Remember to discuss this with the planner in advance. If there's no appropriate person to hold your signs, you don't want to count on that! And, by all means, plan on bringing them yourself, made on or glue-sticked onto good card stock. If you laminate them, you're more likely to get multiple uses from them.

Having a timekeeper is an easy way to stay on schedule without using clocks.

8. Use watches carefully.

Watches are the least clunky solution as they easily fit on your arm before you leave home and they are always with you. The problem with them is that, while it's easy to take a quick look at a clock or a timekeeper without being noticeable, it's not as easy to look at your watch without it being seen.

Who cares if they see it? Well, it's a reminder to them that time is passing and then they start to wonder what time it is, how much longer it will be, whether they've gotten any voicemail, etc. You want the time to be seamless to them.

So how do you pull this off well if it's tricky? In spite of the challenges and while it's not the best solution for everyone, I do favor my watch over bringing clocks or timekeepers. Just a personal choice – not better or worse.

Here are a couple of tips you can use for less-noticeable watch checking:

- Looking at your watch takes two steps — rolling up the edge of your sleeve and looking at the face. You can break this up to make the sneak-peak less noticeable by pushing up your sleeve while speaking but *not* looking at your watch at that moment. Then, ten or fifteen seconds later, you can glance at your wrist less noticeably.

- If you really just need to look at your watch in the latter half, do the fake-cough-watch-look or simply be honest and acknowledge the peek in a positive way ("How are we doing on time? Oh, good, we're fine." – even if you're not, because you're gonna MAKE it fine for them using your other pacing skills.)

Interactive time is also a great chance to check your timepiece because the focus is off of you.

---

9. **Have a couple of stories late in the speech that can be told in a much shorter version or cut completely.**

My "Screw Up of the Month" story takes about four minutes to tell well with all the fun details. But I also have a version that I can tell in about 40 seconds. It lacks the laughs, theatrics, and specifics that make the story as memorable. When time is pressed, though, it makes the same point, gains me back three minutes, and (since I'm still telling the story to some degree) it means I don't have to skip a PowerPoint slide. That always makes an audience wonder what they just missed out on.

Likewise, my final slide has a graphic and a few words that lend themselves to a nice closing story. If time is running over, I use the same graphic and words to leave them with a final thought instead of a story. Only *I* know something was missing!

---

10. Use your website for more information.

Running out of time and you have some facts that you normally share? Have them on your website with a direct link in the handout or write it large on something. Then you get to say something like:

"Everything we've discussed today about writing your non-fiction book will leave you ready to look into *publishing* your material. That's more of a topic than we have time for today, but if you look at www.MiloShapiro.com/resources, I've posted some interesting information just for you about this final step."

Sure, it would be better if you could discuss it, but you're still meeting their needs better than skipping the information entirely, you've caught up on time, and you've even given them a reason to go to your site!

"Gee, Milo, all of this information is great, but I feel like I'm all alone in working on it all. Isn't there some way for me to feel supported so I know I'm on the right track?"

Absolutely...and it's important! Comedians write jokes and they have no idea if anyone else will find them funny until they test them on others. Likewise, writing and rehearsing spoken material can be a lonely and frustrating process, leaving you wondering if you're making progress or wasting time. Your friends and family are too biased to be really helpful — if they'll even listen to you for as long as you'd need!

To this end, there are two great solutions: Toastmasters and coaching. There are benefits to each — enough so that it bears a chapter with nine points on why Toastmasters can be helpful and with one final one on why a coach might still be the right solution in some cases.

22

10 Superb Reasons To Join Toastmasters or Hire a Speaking Coach

Toastmasters International is an amazing organization dedicated to improving communication and leadership skills. Most clubs meet weekly and, depending on the length of the meetings, two to five members get to give a short, prepared speech then evaluated by other members.

In this chapter, I'll give you nine reasons why I think Toastmasters is great and reserve one point on why sometimes a coach is the right solution for some people's needs instead.

1.   Tried and true.

If Toastmasters were ineffective, they wouldn't have enrolled between three and four *million* members in 90 countries, all learning and growing with them since 1924.

2.   Support of a group.

Everyone in a Toastmasters club was new to it at some point so they are sincerely supportive of new members and the issues they are facing.

You can find your closest club (and more information about this educational non-profit organization) at www.Toastmasters.org.

3. Sense of routine.

Knowing you have a Toastmasters routine (like scheduling those 60-90 minutes with your local club every Tuesday at 11:30 am) makes public speaking a part of your life instead of a separate issue.

4. Learn from the critiques of others.

While it's fine to rehearse to your cat, you're probably not going to get constructive feedback (at best a yawn, which is not particularly motivating).

At Toastmasters, you will get kind, candid feedback on how you did with content and delivery from one or two real human people in your club — no cats allowed!

5. Variety of people giving feedback.

Each week, the roles of speaker, meeting facilitator, and speech evaluator are rotated. So while Mary might have been evaluating your "ice breaker" speech, Jose might evaluate your "how to persuade" speech. Over time, you'll hear from a number of people, though you won't speak at every meeting.

6. Exposure to a lot of different styles.

Quite a bit of learning happens as we watch others speak, struggle, excel, and get evaluated. You'll gain insight that will help you even on the weeks where you don't say anything more than hello, or introduce yourself to the group.

Learn from watching the speaking styles of others.

Hmm...that may work for him but I don't quite think it's me...

7. Inexpensive.

There are nominal semi annual membership dues and clubs offer a chance to check out 2-3 meetings as their guest. It's quite an affordable way to learn when you have the time to put into getting your money's worth (like most things in life, if you don't go, you won't get much value from your membership!).

8. Social as well.

Toastmasters brings out lively, supportive people who are usually eager to give back to new people in return for the help they've been given along the way. And yes, they'll expect the same positive, helpful spirit from you — especially as you, too, become an evaluator or a mentor for others in the group.

---

9. Speaking on the fly.

Toastmasters has a special portion of the meeting agenda called "Table Topics." This is a chance for a few people to participate who were not *scheduled* to speak otherwise that day.

The person in charge, the Table Topics Master, selects a theme and writes several open-ended questions that are posed to attendees. After a few seconds for thinking time, the leader randomly picks a member (or an eager, courageous guest) to answer the question.

For instance, the Table Topics Master might say, "This week in the news, the President talked about the need for Americans to save for retirement. Please tell us about your efforts or challenges in budgeting your income... Phyllis?" Then Phyllis gets to stand up and choose, perhaps, to talk about her 401k and how she's started bringing her lunch to cut back on restaurant bills.

The intention of the exercise is to practice addressing a random topic, speaking off the top of your head, and making your point in the prescribed time (usually 30-45 seconds), as if answering a question during a Q&A section in a meeting or interview.

Speaking off the cuff is a great skill to have and Table Topics is an easy, fun way to practice the skill.

---

10. Why one might hire a speaking coach instead of (or in addition to) Toastmasters

This could almost be a top-ten list of its own, but I'll resist the temptation!

The fact is that Toastmasters is a great organization from which I benefited greatly. I joined for general speaking improvement, not because there was a specific program I wanted to improve at giving or a specific set of issues I wanted to overcome.

Toastmasters has done a brilliant job in creating their all-encompassing program that, when followed, leads to improvement in communication skills. Coaching, by contrast, is customized to focus more tightly upon meeting an individual's specific needs, goals, and interests.

For instance, in just the last three months, separate clients came to me with these varied concerns (I've included my very different responses and coaching for each):

- Frustration at his inability to memorize his opening. <u>Coaching response</u>: Taking him through a process that links ideas so the memorization became fun and logical.
- Not speaking clearly enough that everyone can understand him. <u>Coaching response</u>: Working on vocal exercises that help him practice his challenge letters (the same way I taught myself to tone my thick New York accent way down).
- Trying to come up with a more powerful way to introduce herself at networking meetings so that people would remember her. <u>Coaching response</u>: Helping her figure out what made her services unique and then creating carefully worded statements to convey the message powerfully.
- Improving the same program she'd been working on for weeks because it had to be fantastic when given. <u>Coaching response</u>: Running that same program again each week with new focuses as she improves different aspects.
- Fear of making a presentation to the parents of the children she works with. <u>Coaching response</u>: Creating a program for the parents that would still convey the facts, but using her strengths to get her there.
- Struggling to gain comfort with a stilted introduction that was awkward and dragging. <u>Coaching response</u>: Writing an introduction together that *was* less stilted, included a bit of humor, and felt more authentically "him."
- Helping him figure out what he wanted to focus on when being asked to motivate a group. <u>Coaching response</u>: Discussing the stories of his life to see what lessons had been strongest and created the most positive turns for him.

Can you think of a way *all* of these needs could have been met by a *single* program? Coaching is a streamlined, powerful shortcut compared to public programs...because coaching is all about dealing with what YOU need NOW.

The better you get at speaking, the more valuable it becomes in your life and the more places you will see to use it to your advantage. For most people, simply being better at it is enough. For others, they crave the chance to do it publicly and share a message...or perhaps build a career on speaking on that message.

Let's look at how you can get out of your living room and in front of groups who need to hear what you have to say. And we'll talk turkey, too...unless you'd prefer to be paid in cash than poultry!

23

10 Steps to Making the Leap to *Getting* Speeches

A certain percentage of any audience watching a paid, professional speaker is thinking: "I could do that. That looks easy. Why would I want to go to my job every day when I could just get up in front of groups, speak for an hour, and make more in that hour than I do all day?"

Hopefully, having read up to this point in the book, you've seen that this is *not* an easy process to perfect and that, if the speaker *has* managed to make it look easy, he has really earned his fee! Not to mention the countless hours that lead up to *getting* that speaking engagement.

Unless you're a celebrity already, it's unlikely you're going to make the immediate leap from wanting to speak to having paid bookings just waiting for you. So let's look at steps that will help the process so you can start marketing yourself...and know that the money factor will become part of the equation along the way...in the *next* chapter!

1.   Take a class in improvisation.

My improv training has helped me more than anything else I've done in this field to be ready to try material in different ways, adapt to changes, customize material for new clients, and many other applications.

While the novice may not see the connection or may focus on the funny-vs.-not-funny factor they associate with improv, improv is about training your brain to respond quickly, build on the ideas of others (or the last thing you said), and handle change with grace.

Treat yourself to some laughs and learning by finding out where there is an improv beginner class near you. You can look in the arts classified section of your paper, check local colleges or adult-education programs, or even contact an improv troupe in your city (who are bound to know what training is in town...if they don't offer it themselves!)

---

2.   **Contact NSA.**

While nothing helped me more than improv in being ready to *do* professional speaking, nothing has helped me more in being ready for the *business* of professional speaking than the **National Speakers Association**. This national organization (which can be found via www.nsaSpeaker.org) has so much to offer and was founded specifically to support those in the speaking industry and those wanting to be in it.

In addition to the national organization's resources and programs for those new to the business, the local chapters are probably your best place to start! Local chapters may or may not be physically near you; some states share a chapter while other states have multiple chapters. Use the national website to find out which one is closest and what programs they have for novices.

Many chapters welcome those interested at their larger meetings. Some even have "apprentice programs" or special events just for novices, designed to help those transitioning from "wannabe" to marketing themselves.

Without my local chapter of NSA and the support of the people within it, I can say with 100% certainty that there is no chance I'd be in the industry today; that's how important they were in my learning and action.

3. Subscribe to SpeakerNetNews.

SpeakerNetNews is like the "Hints from Heloise" of the speaking industry. The amazing volunteer editors of this free resource request that recipients pay their "dues" by submitting at least two tips per year that others can learn from. Of course, if you're new and don't have something to share yet, they won't hold that against you.

Weekly, you'll receive easy short tips that other speakers have discovered on topics like:

- Technology
- Negotiating
- Better use of props and timing
- Printing information
- Data resources
- Attention-getters

....and many more. Some of it may be beyond your stage of development right now (some of the tips are still way past anything *I'm* even doing yet) but I always read each issue in full and save it to my files so I have access to them I'm ready for ideas that relate to them.

To subscribe, visit www.SpeakerNetNews.com. As of the time of this printing, it's free and I expect it will stay that way. You'll see some advertising in it for some great teleseminars you might want to take – that's classes where the teacher has everyone call in and you learn over the phone.

---

4. Get "Speaker" magazine.

Until recently, I thought only NSA members could get "Speaker" magazine because it's produced by the NSA. As it turns out, anyone can subscribe to this quality publication devoted purely to the art and business of speaking.

It is available on NSA's website: www.nsaSpeaker.org.

---

5. Get clarity on what the message of your first speech will be!!!

Note the *three* exclamation points because this is so essential!

One of my trickiest tasks as a coach is when I get someone who comes to me and says, "I love speaking and people tell me I'm a good speaker. I'd like to pursue that as a career." When I ask what they intend to speak on, I've heard anything from "Well, I just don't know yet" to "Oh, I can speak on anything; what do you think I should speak on?"

It's important to remember that all of the skillful expression, passionate storytelling, and vocal variety we work on is all geared for one purpose: to convey the message. Without that, we are just performing.

Be clear what <u>your</u> speaking message is.

Your highest priority regarding the topic of your first speech is choosing something that makes *sense* for you to speak on. By sense, I mean that there may very well be a need for people to speak on sexual harassment in the workplace, but if you have no background in this area and/or the topic has little interest for you, leave it to someone well-trained and passionate about the subject!

You are looking for a topic that is well-suited to your background and which you feel strongly enough about that you could talk about this every day for a year...and *still* look forward to the *next* chance to share it.

Remember that if your first speech is successful, your second and third could be on either other aspects of your *original* topic (e.g.: more detailed knowledge, other ways of looking at it) or complementary topics (e.g.: workplace sexual harassment followed by workplace violence *prevention*, followed by conflict negotiation). This is called finding a **niche** or, as the industry has coined the phrase, **"niching"** yourself.

After you have gone through all the work to be known as a good speaker in the niche of "Customer Service", you can get return clients. For instance, once you've proven yourself on that topic with your speech "Customer Service in Your Store", it becomes a lot easier to return to them with your new program "Customer Service on the Phone" than to sell them on you as a speaker about "Marketing Trends." No matter how versatile you *could* be, in their minds, you're that guy/gal that they recommended to colleagues for their "Customer Service" program; marketing is not how they know you. It also looks like you're trying to be everything to everyone instead of becoming an **expert** in one area. And people want to hire experts.

There are numerous speaking categories, but for me, they all seem to fall into three more general categories (though they can overlap):

- **Informational** - leaving your audience with important facts that they need
- **Motivational** - conveying a thought that will inspire your audience to do something differently in their work or life
- **Entertainment** - making the time they spend with you as enjoyable as possible, regardless of whether there is information or a message

Again, there IS overlap and I certainly hope all of your programs are entertaining; the question is whether you are being seen *as* entertainment. For instance, sex therapist Dr. Ruth draws a good number of laughs when she gives speeches because she is a funny, high energy keynoter...but no one hires her to *be* an entertainer.

There is nothing better about one of these than another, but they will market differently. Informational are the easiest to market to **corporate** - they often affect revenue in directly measurable ways (e.g.; sales, efficiency, management) or fulfill legal requirements (e.g.; sexual harassment, diversity, safety).

Corporate will sometimes hire motivational or entertainment speakers if they feel it will help in some area or make their full day program more interesting overall, but there is also a strong target audience in **professional associations**, who frequently need speakers for their periodic events.

When you know what you want to talk about, ask yourself which of the three categories best fits your program. While it's great to include aspects of the other two, it will help you focus on why you are there.

---

6. **Outline your program and begin rehearsing.**

The time to put your program together is *not* when you've got someone interested in using your services. For newcomers, this may be tempting because there is the fear that "I'll be wasting my time if they are looking for something different!" Unlikely.

More likely, you will accomplish two things by starting ASAP to outline, write, and rehearse:

a. You will have far greater clarity in what your program looks like, enabling you to speak about it in a more focused and confident manner. This WILL help you find audiences; no one wants to discover a wishy-washy description when they are searching for a speaker.

b. You'll be creating (consciously or not) sections that can be removed, rearranged, replaced, and tweaked such that preparing for that first client will be an exercise in **customizing**, not creating. While few speakers love customizing (because we fall in love with our base programs), you'll quickly learn that it's way easier to customize an existing program than create a new one from scratch.

---

7. Create a one-sheet.

The industry standard for sending out information is something called a **one-sheet**. It is essentially a flyer to get them interested in you. Let's discuss the key aspects of a one-sheet individually:

a. Basic Format

It is just one sheet of paper! It can be printed on either one side of the sheet OR both sides. The latter is just as acceptable and gives you twice the space to work with, but professional printing is not cheap. Given the choice between a quality one-sider or a homemade two-sider, quality wins out. PDF files are a speaker's best friend because they are easy to create from Word or Publisher, look the same on every computer, and can be printed by most professional print shops.

b. Features

A one-sheet should include:

- Your contact information – full name, email address, phone number, mailing address, and your professional website (if you have one; don't share that free one you made with the pictures of your last vacation).

- Your primary topic(s) –descriptions of what you speak on and/or titles of the presentations that you do.

- Testimonials - Short powerful quotes from satisfied clients (if you have these yet), especially valued if any of the names are recognizable, but it still looks good to see:

> "Our attendees left buzzing with new ideas they wanted to implement!"
>
> - Jim Ruboyianes, Ohio Fabrics Association

Even if they have no idea who that person is!

- <u>A partial client history list</u> – this is a way of getting those big names you've worked with onto the page without having to quote each one. If you don't have such a list yet, you can use more quotes instead and hopefully it'll look like a style choice instead of a lack of experience.

  ("But, Milo!" some readers cry, "I haven't spoken to anyone yet! I've got no one to quote **or** list!" The answer is to hold off a bit on designing your first one-sheet and find some groups that will trust you to speak based on conversations you have with them. Let them know you're happy to speak for free if they'll just give you a testimonial letter afterward.)

- <u>Photo(s)</u> - a professional, flattering photo or two of yourself is valuable. People like to see who they are getting and put a face to the information or voice on the phone.

  Depending how you design it, anything from a headshot to a full body shot can be used successfully, but what's important is that they see your face clearly and in good scale size. So, if you're going to go with a full body shot, it's probably going to take up a lot of your precious space. Of course, if you haven't much to say, that could be used to your advantage.

  In general, you *do* want to hire a good photographer for this, especially if you can find one who specializes in marketing photos. This is not Glamour Shots; your shot should say "professional, likeable, and interesting", not "a good time on a Saturday night."

c. Layout

Point blank: This ain't easy. There's a lot of things you can do right and wrong in a one-sheet but I will give you one lesson that I learned the hard and expensive way: Less is more! Ever so easy to say but painfully difficult to implement.

I mean, this is your passion, right? You want to use the smallest font, cover every inch of both sides, and describe everything so well that they just HAVE to hire you, right?

Oh so very wrong! The perfect one-sheet should contain everything that a meeting planner would need to make her want to call you for more information. Note that this is *not* the same thing as containing everything a meeting planner could possibly want to know about you before deciding to hire you.

There is a reason that careers exist in graphic design and copy editing. It is both an art and a business to know how to take a concept, person, business, or product and make it come to life on a published sheet. A bad one-sheet could actually undermine a good conversation that you've had with someone.

I really recommend finding someone who does this professionally — preferably someone who has done it for other speakers and knows the speaking business. If you contact your local NSA chapter, it is likely that, through them, you can find someone in your area that other speakers have used. It's fine to use someone out of town, but it's better if you can meet them and have them get a sense of your energy. They may also have photographers they like to work with, if you haven't done that step yet.

Of course, no matter how much I encourage you to have it done professionally, some people simply aren't going to take that step right now. If that's you, here are a couple of recommendations:

- San Diego-based professional speaker and graphic design expert Sheryl Roush helps people design brochures like these. Not only does she help people put these together and review existing material on a consulting basis, but she has DVDs with model examples that can help you to do it yourself. Learn more about her options and teaching tools at www.SparklePresentations.com.

- Get Microsoft Publisher and Adobe Acrobat. Publisher currently comes with the "Professional" version of Microsoft Office. Acrobat is a fairly inexpensive download from Adobe, who makes the free "Adobe Reader" that you probably already use to look at PDFs.

  The industry standards are currently tools like Quark, InDesign, and Adobe Illustrator. Prior to the versatility of the PDF, you needed to use these complicated tools to create brochures because their files were accepted by print shops which the highly-intuitive, easy-to-learn MS Publisher was not. But now, thanks to the PDF, most print shops can and will print from a PDF you email or upload to them.

  The only problem is that, as of today, MS Publisher does not offer the option to save a file as a PDF. That's where Adobe Acrobat comes in with almost NO learning curve. Upon installation of Acrobat, you will have the option to "print" a file to Adobe instead of your printer and *voila*: You have a PDF of your brochure.

  Microsoft Publisher is a lot like Word but it's much more photo-friendly. Ever try to move a photo around in MS Word and all your text starts moving into places you hadn't intended? That's what's great about MS Publisher. You put your text in as text-boxes and they stay where you put them even as you move pictures and other text-boxes around.

- Microsoft Word, frustrating as it can be for layout, has come a long way in its flexibility. And, best of all, you can turn Word files into PDFs now – either with a single click using Adobe Acrobat or by using one of a number of free online tools or sites that convert Word to PDF for you.

Why is it so important to turn documents into PDFs? Because, no matter how common the tool — even Word — there are differences between computers. Even if you're lucky enough that the recipient can open files of your type, it might display them reformatted just enough that it'll make your document a mess. But PDF is universal. It will look the same on every machine, so you can send them with confidence.

Of course, if you're only going to print them, you needn't convert them at all. But I try not to print anything I can email! Faster, cheaper, usually sharper looking, and easier for the recipient to share!

---

8.   Contact service clubs and HR departments.

Service clubs are always looking for people to speak and it's a great place to try out your material in short timeframes without putting your reputation too much on the line. Be honest with them about the fact that it's a new program and that you're an aspiring speaker. They may not pay, but they are still an audience who deserve to be treated respectfully. You can even say that you're hoping to receive feedback from some of them to better your delivery. Not only will you get interesting food-for-thought, but they'll be more attentive since they are now charged with a reason to be engaged.

HR departments in small companies occasionally bring in presenters; can't hurt to ask. In larger companies, HR won't be able to get you in with work groups, but sometimes they'll organize "Lunch and Learn" classes. This is where employees are encouraged to bring a bag lunch to spend their lunch hour learning from you. If your topic is one that the company thinks has value and they haven't considered it before,, you might even be able to suggest it. Being innovative can create opportunities for you to speak that might not have been on the table before.

---

9.   Collect every possible referral letter.

This is one of the most overlooked promotional opportunities and I've seen so many speakers wish they had started it sooner. While the bigger the company/organization name, the more likely that you'll want to quote their letter, you never know which speech's testimonial will be the right one to have.

Key rule of starting in speaking: *Speak anywhere and everywhere you can for free to build up a file of referral letters.* Do not leave this to fate. Say to them right up front, "One of my conditions for speaking is that, if you are satisfied that I did a good job, you will provide a letter of reference for my records. Is that okay?" Almost everyone will say yes. After the event, you ask them, "Did you feel that went well?" If the answer is no, better that you know! If the answer is yes, you get to say, "Oh, I'm so glad. Then I'll be in touch by email to ask you for the testimonial letter we discussed." Be prepared to remind them Once you're done speaking, you're no longer a priority. But do follow up...why did you invest your time if there's nothing in it for you?

Initially, you might think, "Do I really need a letter from the American Button Association? Nah...I've got better ones." But you'll be really sorry you didn't ask for it when the American Zipper Association calls and the programs are so similar. People tend to look at your previous clients partly to be impressed but also, in part, to see if you've worked with a group similar to theirs.

Initially, my press pack had letters from some pretty small-chaptered organizations like Lions, Kiwanis, Optimists, and Rotary. Then I moved up to opportunities with local chapters of professional groups, like the International Society of Performance Improvement, the Project Management Association, and San Diego Accounting Day. I spoke to interesting, supportive people in each case, but you can already see how the latter group would look better for quotes.

Eventually, companies like Southwest Airlines, Pfizer, and Kodak replaced many of the organizations on my one-sheet, but I still keep a few professional societies on there to show that I'm happy to serve that market, too (and the checks cash the same way).

---

10. Give referrals to others.

You can tell other speakers what you do until you're blue in the face, but the best way to get other speakers to refer you is to refer *them*.

After you give a program, ask the coordinator if there are other themes he'll be tackling this year. If you have the chance to give another speaker's name (or better yet, to ask if it might be okay for your colleague to contact him), do it! That speaker will remember you for it. It's good networking, baby.

Okay, I said we'd talk turkey and money wasn't mentioned in this chapter. But really, getting out there for experience and exposure is a major step in the right direction.

Still, I promised a money-talk chapter, so let's move into a whole chapter on the *business* of speaking.

24

10 Steps to Making the Leap to Getting *Paid* for Speeches

Ah, the joy of getting paid for something you enjoy doing (and if you don't enjoy doing it, it really ain't gonna be worth how hard you're going to have to work to make it happen!)

How does one transition from doing some speaking to being a professional speaker (i.e.: getting paid). Well, for good or for bad, there is no equivalent in public speaking to a lawyer passing her bar exam or a school teacher getting his teaching credential. There *is* a designation called a CSP (Certified Speaking Professional) that is offered by NSA, but it requires *such* a high level of experience that most members of NSA never reach it, even if they are very good and are charging high fees. The reality is that anyone can ask for a fee for speaking and the only thing that can stop him from receiving it is whether or not there's someone on the receiving end willing to pay it.

This makes it easier for beginning speakers to get out there, but tougher on experienced ones who can't show their training credential. This is why testimonials, years in service, referrals and membership in the NSA become so important (especially in this day and age where *anyone* can put up a website and declare themselves a speaker).

Most people who are going to pay anything substantial are sharp enough to ask to see referrals, printed materials, website pages, and possibly video samples. This is their way of gauging your experience as best they can, since there is no accreditation they can use.

So let's look at ten things you can do, once you've gotten some experience speaking for free, to move toward being a paid speaker instead.

---

1.   Know your fee.

Aaaa! The scariest part of it all. What's enough? What's too much? If you've been thinking this, you're in good company. Even the professionals lose sleep over this one, be it raising their rates from $100 to $150 or from $8000 to $10,000.

There's no way I can tell you what you should charge. I can tell you that main factors you should consider are:

- How expert are you on the topic?
- How well are you known on your topic?
- How many times you have delivered this speech or one like it?
- From whom do you have testimonials?
- How much competition you would have for this opportunity to speak?
- Have you spoken for *this* group before?
- How much customizing would be required?
- How good do you believe (and hear) you are?
- How sharp are your marketing materials?
- How far away is the event?

Be prepared for what you'll accept. And hardest of all, be willing to pass up work when they won't meet your price. You'll be surprised how many times they come back after rethinking it, if you really are a good fit. But you have to let some go.

As a friend once said to me, "Would you rather speak to one group that met your price or three groups that would pay 1/3? If you charge the 1/3 price, the one who *would* have paid three times that amount never will."

That doesn't mean you have to start out high. You might actually choose a small number like $50 at first simply to establish that your time has some value. You have plenty of time to raise it. I've known numerous speakers who have said that that first check for $25 or so meant far more to them than checks for thousands did later in their careers.

Some groups will simply say, "We don't pay for speakers." They think they are doing you a favor somehow letting you speak. Initially, that may have been true, but if you're moving toward charging, ask yourself "Why would I be willing to do that?" There may indeed be an answer (i.e.: it's for a cause you'd support; it'd be the best referral letter you've gotten so far) but often there's no good reason...so pass! Let it be their loss.

If you really want a job and they simply cannot pay (some groups have it in their charter that they are not allowed to pay speakers), ask if there's anything non-monetary you could receive to make up the difference. This could be advertising, publicity, referrals, or even goods or services. One speaker I know had a group that only had a small budget, but had access to a new PDA that they could throw in. She was thrilled to do it for what was cutting edge technology of its time. An airline once paid me with enough flight vouchers to make it worthwhile.

2. Read up on sales negotiation.

Make no mistake about it: This is a business. Few will recognize the time and costs that go into marketing, research, preparation, travel, coordination, customization, and rehearsal. To them, you are working just an hour for your fee. *You* know how much more is involved.

Sales negotiation is a huge topic that is beyond the scope of this book, but I encourage you to read, listen, and seek help to get good at this awkward but crucial dance of business. Making one right move (or avoiding one *wrong* approach) will make such training invaluable.

3. Think of yourself and introduce yourself as a speaker.

This is more about a mindset than about marketing, but half of selling your speech is selling yourself. At the point where you are marketing your services, you need to think of yourself as a professional speaker.

If you were previously:

- Unemployed
- A homemaker
- A student
- Part time anything

that is no longer what you tell people when they ask what you do. You can now answer "I'm a professional speaker who focuses on _____". If they *continue* to get to know you, then you can tell them about your children or your masters program or your double shift at Starbucks (where you *happen* to enjoying doing a couple of shifts each week for extra money between speeches).

Likewise, if you have full-time job, your reply should be along the lines of:

"I'm sales rep for Plainview Carpets and I'm also a motivational speaker on how to boost sales."

Why? Which do think is the more likely response:

1) "Really! I've always been interested in carpet sales!"
2) "Really! Who do you talk to about sales and what do you teach them?"

The latter, of course. And it's in *your* best interest that the conversation *should* go that way because you need to start telling people whenever possible. You never know when someone will have a connection you didn't expect. This has paid off for me more times than I can mention.

---

4. **Have a "business" line.**

Ideally, you'll want to have a separate phone line that you can answer appropriately. If you choose to make it your cell line, that's fine...so long as you don't mind being accessible 24/7. The important thing is that there be a number that you can answer, "Good morning, Jonathan Price's office." If you develop a business name (easily and not expensively registered at your city hall), that's even better: "Good morning, Price Sales Solutions."

If you have no other employees, make sure you're the only one to answer that phone. Better that the caller get your voicemail (which will also sound like a business), than to get the seven year old screaming, "Mom...someone on the phone for you!" This does not sound like a business.

If you live alone, you might make your only line serve both business and personal...so long as you always answer it as a business. Your friends may tease you at first about sounding so professional on your home or cell line, but better to explain it to friends than to have a potential client call and get, "Hello?"

And remember: It doesn't matter if you're answering in your pajamas with hair sticking up everywhere, if you sound professional, that's what they'll hear.

Unless you can sound fully professional in your home-based office, let it ring through to voicemail.

5.   Get business cards.

If you are a speaker, you need to be able to offer a business card that tells people what you speak on and how to reach you.

For only a *little* more money, you can get cards with your face and even a logo on it. This is money well-spent. I can rarely remember who gave me which card at the end of a night of networking, but if there's a face on the card, our whole conversation comes back to me.

The costs have dropped dramatically, especially if you order on the net. I've seen 2500 double-sided cards in full color for under $100. Make the investment in something that will reflect so positively upon you. If people say, "Nice card!", you've made an impression.

---

6.   Create a website.

In the 21st Century, there is no getting around the need for a website. It'll be the first thing almost any perspective client will want to see. Even if it's nothing special, seeing it on your card tells them that there *is* a place to get more information without having to call.

How your site should look is again beyond the scope of this book, but you can look at the sites of speakers in the NSA to see a few that you like. As long as you list what you do, what makes you unique, how to reach you, and include a few pictures, you are way ahead of having no site at all. Over time, you can add testimonials, products for sale, articles you've written, and more.

If you cannot manage hosting a site of your own and you need to use on of the free sites that are offered by aol, hotmail, yahoo, etc., then at least invest in a good site name that forwards automatically to the longer name. At the time of this writing, www.GoDaddy.com is offering this feature for all of NINE dollars a year.

So there's no reason to ever give someone a site like:

> www.hometown.aol/users/business/0223.htm

when, for $9, you could have a nice name like:

> www.MichelleAckermanSpeaks.com

that forwards to the one above. Notice how I capitalized each word for clarity. It won't matter if they type caps or not, but it sure reads better that way.

Also, whatever sitename you use, make sure that if they DO type all smalls, it can't be read some way you didn't *intend*. I love the story of how the founders of www.PenIsland.com didn't think out how wrong it would look when it was spelled out in lowercase as www.penisland.com!

---

7. **Create a video.**

A good professionally-filmed, tightly-edited video that gives an overview of what you do and shows you in action can be a huge factor in your getting jobs and being able to command higher fees. People like knowing what they are going to be getting and it's hard to get that in still shots, phone calls, and even audio tapes. Currently, there's nothing stronger than a good 5-7 minute video to showcase yourself.

In only a few short years, the trend has gone from VHS to CD-ROM to DVD to streaming video, so it's difficult for me to tell you what the current demand format will be when you read this, but streaming video on websites is likely to remain strong for quite some time. The bottom line is that formats may vary, but the video itself must be good.

Video production can be expensive; I know one high-fee speaker who spent over $10,000 on her video because she felt it would pay for itself quickly. Few beginning speakers can afford this.

Your local NSA chapter may be able to help you find a good videographer and editor, but in the meantime, get some good digital camcordering of yourself so you can find a nice section within it that you can share, either by mailing it to a potential client or by setting it up for download or streaming on your site.

One hint I love: If it's not too long, you can put it on YouTube and embed the HTML for that video in your site so, except for a little logo in the corner, it looks like it's streaming right on your own site. It's so easy and you'll have streaming video for free with only a few minutes of effort.

---

8. Write articles you can pitch and post.

One of the best ways to get free publicity is to write articles for industry magazines that can be related to your topic. The big magazines are hard to get in with, but I'm betting that "Shoelace Manufacturer's Monthly" is tearing their hair out trying to come up with something they haven't already done for next month's issue.

If you speak on intergenerational learning and can determine that the shoelace industry holds a wide variety of age brackets, they may never have done an article on your topic. It's up to you to write something like:

"Remember when everyone in the shoelace industry was young and hip? Well, that was 1960. Now that some of those folks are top managers in the industry and the new hires could be their great-grandchildren, dealing with generational issues has never been more important to us."

Then you go on with the same stuff you always say about generations. But now you're a fit for their monthly.

Why would you do this for them? Because at the end, they'll put:

> *Wayne Gunnlaugsson is a professional speaker who deals in creating productive, peaceful work teams in multigenerational workplaces. For more on his speeches and trainings, visit www.GenerationGuy.com.*

And you never know who will read that! Or the almost identical article you'll submit to the newsletters for Velcro and ButtonSnap industries...

9. Write the book.

Easier said than done, I know. (*Boy*, do I know...)

But in spite of being part of an ever increasing email/PDF/link-to-information society, there is still prestige to being the author of a book. People continue to hold to the belief that if you've got enough know-how to create a book, you must know more than someone who hasn't done so.

What to write about, how to organize the book, and how/whether to seek a publisher would be the topic of a whole 'nuther book (or twenty). If there's a book inside you, though, and you've been burning to write it (or even if you think you could stomach the writing of it), it's a remarkable tool.

Let's say Miss Mary Meetingplanner is looking for a speaker and is choosing between Alan and Alice, two speakers on time management. Alice's website offers her book "The Time Manager's Bible". Doesn't she seem more intriguing than Alan now? Experience shows us that most meeting planners do think so. Now imagine that Alice sends Mary a free autographed copy...this could be a $5 expense that yields her thousands of dollars, even if Mary never reads past page 5!

10. Create/join a Mastermind group.

A Mastermind group is a group of people with a similar interest or focus, usually at similar levels of experience. At scheduled meetings, each person is given time to share what has been going on for him, what struggles the group might be able to help him with and what discoveries he has made that might be useful to the others.

For example, speaker Jim might say:

> "This month, I've been focusing on writing a second speech so that, when things go well with a client, I can be re-hired by them in the future. I'd love to try out the

introduction on a couple of you later, if I could get some feedback. Also, I've just discovered how powerful the AutoCorrect feature of Word is and how it can be used to put whole blocks of commonly-typed text into letters I write, so I want to do a little demo on that, as well."

It's better if members are at similar points in their ventures because there has to be something in it for everyone – and it's less likely that a newbie is going to have as much to offer an experienced speaker.

Hey, you got through all of the top-ten lists! I bet the idea of speaking in front of groups isn't nearly as daunting to you any more. If you didn't follow my advice to highlight this book as you read it, now would be a great time to leisurely flip though the whole book and highlight just those point headings that you think would be good for you to refer back to. That way, it'll bring back a lot of the memories of reading this book in a hurry when it's time for you to speak.

Guess we're ready for a wrap up…top-ten style, of course!

25

Epilogue (or 10 Final Thoughts on Speaking)

In the long run, while good public speaking skills are important to develop, we often take the significance of almost any particular speech too seriously. Now that you've had the chance to digest the 240 points in this book (many of which will stay with you even if you never re-read), let's take a step back and take a look at the big picture:

1. The outcome of this speech is not going to make-or-break your world. Don't treat the whole thing as more serious than it actually is.

2. Remember that it's about conveying your information well, not about *you* doing well. If you do the first part, the second will naturally follow.

3. People usually relax when they see someone enjoying themselves. It's okay to have fun up there with almost any topic.

4. Remember that the stories you've told repeatedly are new to them. Take your time with them so they hit the mark with each new listener.

5. Rehearse it until you know it so well that you're almost sick of it.

6. Work to get away from your notes, but don't panic if you end up needing them. Just do it as casually and gracefully as you can.

7. Keep in mind that 95% of your audience would never switch places with you, so you already start out with their respect for being up there.

8. You have gifts that have helped you through your life and which have made people care about you; you can bring many of those same gifts to your speeches.

9. Be willing to do your research for facts and stories. It's amazing how quickly we can now find what we want to about our audiences, between the internet and asking the people who are planning the event.

10. EVERYONE messes up sometimes up there. Finding a way to acknowledge and laugh at it with the audience will put it behind you and potentially make you look better than if you'd never made the mistake at all.

If you have a question or would like to learn more about coaching, setting up training, or having me as a motivational speaker at your next event, look me up at www.MiloShapiro.com! It's always great to hear from my readers.

I wish you luck, fun, and great success in all your speaking endeavors.

Milo Shapiro

Appendix A

Check list for planning an event

Here is the current list of questions that I always ask the event planner when preparing for a speaking engagement. As my list probably will differ from yours, I encourage you to visit my website's resource section, copy the current version of this list into your word processor, and customize it for your needs.

- List all relevant contacts for this event, with these four facts:

    Name   Phone   Title   Email

- What group is this event is for?
- What is the date and time that the meeting starts?
- What time would I actually be going on? (note the important distinction!)
- What is the fax number for the contract? (I don't recommend that you email anything with your signature)
- Name of location and exact directions from a major highway.
- Fee
- What length would or could the speech be?
- What are the seating arrangements (tables, rows, U-shape)?
- What is the expected or typical attendance size?
- Is it just a meeting or is a meal included? If so, am I invited to partake? (This may seem odd to ask since they usually feed you, too...but you might end up hungry if they *didn't* plan on that! It's best to know up front.)
- Do you have a lectern for my notes and/or to stand behind? If not, what can be improvised for the speaker?
- Am I at floor level or raised? If raised, do I have easy physical access to the audience for my interactive portion? (i.e. steps in front, side, jumping down, not at all...)

- If >50 people, what are our amplification options?
- Do you have the ability to show a PowerPoint presentation?
- If so, will you provide the PC, the projector, and the screen if we email the file?
- Will there be a remote PowerPoint control?
- Will the client make copies of the handout if it is sent in advance?
- Upon my arrival, with whom should I check in so you know that I'm here and we can get started together? Can I have a cell number to reach this person or someone else at the event in case of emergency?
- Will another session be in progress when I arrive? If so, is there a break before I go on? Will I have access to the room before I'm on stage?
- Who will do my introduction? May I have his email to send it to him in advance?
- Might it be okay for me to record video of the event? Might I bring a guest to run the recording equipment?
- If other planners would like to see me in front of a live audience, would it be acceptable if a few people stood or sat toward the back?
- What else should I know about this event/group?

This might seem like a lot to ask, but is there anything on here that you wouldn't prefer to have answered in advance? Most planners respect the time I take to ask or email these questions up front.

Appendix B

Packing checklist for <u>all</u> travel

For any trip, business or otherwise, I look over this packing list and check off each item as either packed or unneeded. It won't cover every possible thing I could need for that trip, but it ensures that I bring all the basics I could have wanted.

CLOTHING
Shorts	Jeans/Sweats/cas'l pants	Dress Pants
T-shirts	Socks - Dress and casual	Shoes/Sneakers
Dress Shirts/Ties	FlipFlops/Extra Shoes	Swim/Exercise Wear
Underwear	Jackets	Sweaters/Sweat Shirts
Galoshes/Umbrella	Jewelry	Laundry Bag
Sleepwear	Belt	Sunglasses/Hats

TOILETRIES
Basics (toothbrush, etc)	BugSpray	Elec. razor & plug
Towels	Vitamins/Medications	Manual razor & cream
Hair items	Sunscreen	Iron

FOR USE IN TRANSIT
Passport	Travel Tickets	Cash/Trav. Checks
Maps/Directions	Flight Pillow	Phone & contact info
Music/mp3 player	Reading material	Wallet
Food, candy	Keys—home & there	Camera/Pictures

ELECTRONICS
Laptop	PDA	Flash Memory
Phone	Phone charge cord	Phone spare battery

MISCELLANEOUS POSSIBILITIES
Hangers	Business Cards	Alarm Clock
Earplugs	Tissues	Gifts/Things to enjoy
Pillow and case	Flashlight	Sleeping bag/sheets

Appendix C

Packing checklist for speaking

Whether the speaking engagement is local or distant, there are things that you will probably want to remember to bring.

Some items are in both Appendix A *and* B, in case you're using just one list.

GENERAL
- Directions
- Event specification sheet
- Hard copies of:
    - Introduction
    - On-stage notes
    - Handouts
- USB Memory loaded, just in case, with the following:
    - Introduction
    - PowerPoint file
    - Specifications
    - Handouts
    - Contract (in case of any issues or confusion)
- Any admittance passes for their building
- Blank checks for any staff you have to pay
- Water, tea, snacks
- Clothing options or props

TECHNOLOGY
- PowerPoint remote
- Laptop
- Boom-box/CDs you'll play
- Telephone, charged
- Video Recorder / Tape / Tripod / Power (battery or plug)
- PDA
- Extension cords

PROMOTIONAL
- Business Cards
- Brochures for business
- Pad and pad portfolio
- CDs or books you're selling
- Any giveaways
- Signage

Acknowledgements

My endless gratitude to my friends in the National Speakers Association who, on so many levels, made it possible for me to even start such a book, particularly for their aid in editing, research, printing, and more. Special thanks to several colleagues there, including Greg Godek, Karyn Buxman-Godek, Rodger Price, Lenora Billings-Harris, Sheryl Roush, and Joni Wilson.

Incredible support came to me from my immediate family as they volunteered to offer hours of unexpected effort in editing the material and catching dozens of typos.

Every cartoon inside this book was handcrafted by my father Bob, against his better judgment when he considered how much work would be involved. I believe his initial comment was, "I'm not going to do one for every chapter!' And then he surprised me with all that you've seen herein.

My thanks for enduring my endless technology questions, requests for opinion, further editing, and brainstorming with Robert Gunnlaugsson, Jim Ruboyianes, Halli Lorentz, Allison Gaynor, Monique DéJovanee, and Jordan Liberman. Jeff Fleming, thanks for the ongoing Photoshop answers and support.

And finally, to my godson Danny, who inspires me to want to be at my best so that I might be as good a role model as I can. I hope someday, when he's old enough, he'll sit down and read this and say, "Dang...my Uncle Milo wrote this!"

About The Author

Milo Shapiro grew up in the suburban town of Syosset on Long Island in NY. He graduated college from the State University of New York at Albany in the upstate New York.

His Bachelor of Science degree in Computer Science led to fifteen years in the world of Information Technology, from which he learned many of the lessons of the business world that he would later apply to his next career.

During those years that he was a programmer and project manager, he studied the art of improvisation in San Diego, Los Angeles, San Francisco, Edmonton, and Calgary, developing a deep love for both the art and for how valuable its lessons are in day to day life.

In 2000, he left that career to start his own company, "IMPROVentures", with the following goal: Sharing with the world the many ways we can improve both our business and personal skills through the fun and lessons of improvisation.

One need not be any sort of comedian to benefit from learning to play with spontaneity and creativity in this way. The next few pages describe a few of the programs Milo has developed.

Milo now resides in beautiful San Diego, California and, after spending seven years in Albany, he would be perfectly happy if he never saw snow again.

For more on Milo's programs and how to bring him to your event, visit his website:

www.IMPROVentures.com

TEAMprovising™

IMPROVentures first offering was the **teambuilding course** TEAMprovising™, teaching organizations about communication skills and teamwork through the fun and lessons of improvisation.

Improv teaches us about listening skills, building on each others' ideas, non-verbal communication and more. The lessons apply to **sales and client support** just as much as they do within teams.

While playing these "games", attendees have been known to make statements like, "This is what happens in our staff meetings!" or "My client does this to me!"

Milo has shared this "teambuilding-plus" work with organizations as varied as Southwest Airlines, the U.S. Marines, and San Diego Gas & Electric.

Motivational Speaking

In 2001, his connections to the National Speaker Association led to his development of a new second branch of IMPROVentures focused on **keynote speaking** for conferences and events.

Milo's solo keynote, **"You Gotta Fail...To Succeed!"** is a motivational speech about moving past the fear of failure so we can excel.

When we resist expanding our borders because of fear, we deny ourselves *and* the organizations we serve the brilliance that is in each one of us.

What makes the program so memorable is that he gets the entire audience playing a few basic improv games in pairs from their seats. In a way, it's like a mini-teambuilding event within the keynote, but the games he uses here are designed to make points about risk-taking while allowing everyone to remain in the safety of the audience space.

Letters of reference recommending this program can be found at www.IMPROVentures.com, including praise from Hilton Hotels, Minolta, Southwest Airlines, and Wellpoint/BlueCross insurance.

Business-y Entertainment

In response to requests for **entertainment with a business message**, Milo collaborated to create a keynote duo called "The IMPROVfessionals" who perform a two-person "keynote".

The duo performs ten improv games, each of which is designed to prove a business point on a topic relating to this audience. This "edu-tainment" show has tackled topics including management and teamwork, sales, customer service, communication, event planning, and fundraising.

The response to this program has been wonderful, with managers often saying "We'll remember these lessons because it was so much fun learning them."

Testimonials from Pfizer, Cox Communications, Kodak, Sempra Energy, and Meeting Professionals International can be found on his site: www.IMPROVentures.com.

Public Dynamics

A third branch of IMPROVentures called **"Public Dynamics"** was created by request of some of Milo's clients in other areas. He now offers **classes and coaching in public speaking**, building upon the ideas in the public-speaking top-ten lists used in this book through more personal contact.

One of Milo's clients went on to break all of his personal sales records on the QVC television sales network after Milo's coaching regarding how to work the interview process better to come across more likeable. In particular, by telling better stories more effecttively instead of focusing on details, the client became more compelling on screen.

Milo is also available to deliver keynote speeches on public speaking and the power of *story* to convey a more lasting message.

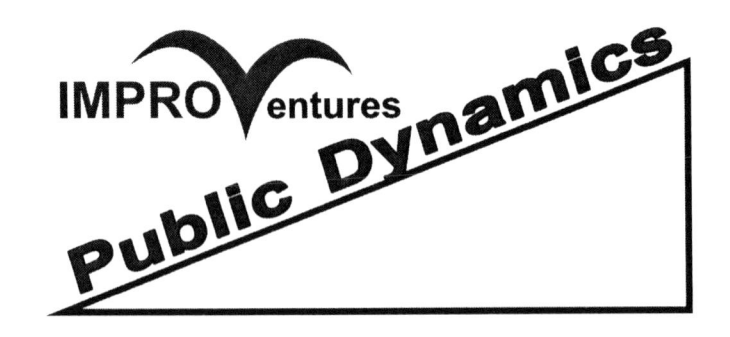

About The Illustrator

Bob Teitelbaum is a former New York lawyer and real estate broken who, now retired to Florida with his wife Joan, has the opportunity to pursue his interests in the arts.

His productions include intensely researched wooden ship models, stained class windows, oil paintings, and photography (both realistic and computer enhanced). This book is his first venture into the world of cartooning.

He's also one heck of a Dad.